# PREDICTABILITY TO CHAOS??

*HOW JEWISH LEADERS REINVENTED THEIR NATIONAL COMMUNAL SYSTEM*

**Gerald B. Bubis**
**Steven F. Windmueller**

**Center for Jewish Community Studies**

**March 2005**
**Adar Bet 5765**

Published by
**Center for Jewish Community Studies**
(An affiliate of the Jerusalem Center for Public Affairs)
5800 Parks Heights Avenue
Baltimore, MD 21215
Phone: (410) 664-5222
Fax: (410) 664-1228
Website: www.cjcs.net

Includes bibliography references.
ISBN: 0-615-12750-9
1999 merger and formation of United Jewish Communities

# TABLE OF CONTENTS

Preface.................................................................................................2
Acknowledgements..............................................................................5
Methodology........................................................................................8
The Interviews...................................................................................10
Introduction.......................................................................................15
Historical Context.............................................................................17
Road To Merger.................................................................................22
Interview Results By Organizational Affiliation................................25
Incorporating The Diversity Of Responses: Professionals And
Themes...............................................................................................55
Perceptions On Process.....................................................................56
Examining Cultural And Institutional Disconnects............................59
Creating Classifications....................................................................65
Institutional Loss – The Five C's.....................................................71
The Perceived Losers.........................................................................74
Winners..............................................................................................78
Overview Comments..........................................................................81
Jewish Values, Social Trends, and Business Practice.......................83
Reflections On Chaos.........................................................................87
Recommendations..............................................................................88
Closing Words..................................................................................112
Appendices.......................................................................................114
Appendix I--List Of Respondents.....................................................115
Appendix II--National Consultation On The UJC Study....................118
Appendix III--Identifying New Opportunities...................................129
Appendix IV--The Literature On Mergers And Collaboration...........134
Appendix V--Introduction To The Ketarim Model.............................142
Appendix VI--The Kehilla Model......................................................145
Appendix VII--History Of Schools Of Jewish Communal Service.......147
Epilogue...........................................................................................148
Biography Of Authors.......................................................................149
References And Bibliography............................................................151
Index.................................................................................................165

# *PREFACE*

Until 1999, the Council of Jewish Federations (CJF), United Jewish Appeal (UJA) and United Israel Appeal (UIA) served as the primary North American umbrella and roof organizations. Collectively, they were responsible for overseeing, advising, aiding and/or monitoring nearly a billion dollars annually in fund raising proceeds and Jewish community services and programs. They were the exclusive repositories of significant holdings of local community foundations.

The creation of United Jewish Communities (UJC) in 1999 was an historic event. Within the Jewish nonprofit sector, it was the single largest reorganization of its kind in the 20th century. It resulted in the largest consolidation of Jewish communal resources ever undertaken. Quite possibly, the merger of the CJF, UJA, and UIA was the most significant in size and scope in American nonprofit history.

The merger reflected two dominant themes: the interest of UJA's leadership in more efficient fundraising, and the federations' desire to have more control over the amount and utilization of funds directed to Israel.

The UJC is in its infancy. Therefore, we use an ethnographic approach to study the merger; there are nuances to this approach that cannot be captured through a quantitative research design. We interviewed those most directly involved in the merger efforts, probing them regarding their own motives and perceptions as to how the process unfolded, how they assessed what took place as the new organization emerged, and their satisfaction with the outcomes to date.

Those interviewed were volunteers and professionals, active in CJF, UJA, UIA, major federations, religious and Zionist streams and representatives of the American Jewish Joint Distribution

Committee (JDC), a principal within the communal system that did not participate in the merger. Our aim was to identify and interview a representative selection of those who were central to the merger process. A great majority of respondents were involved in the various committees and structures established to explore the feasibility and then the implementation of the merger. In addition, we interviewed a random selection of federation executives and presidents who were not directly involved in the merger discussions but had a distinct interest in the outcome. Finally, we interviewed other knowledgeable observers who, although no longer active in any of the three organizations, brought a wealth of experience and insight to the study.

The majority of the 88 interviews were conducted by phone, ranging in duration from one-half hour to two hours. Of all of the prospective individuals we spoke with, only one declined. One was unable to respond because of poor health. While we did not reach a few "key" people due to our own schedules or their availability, we did talk to over 90% of those actively engaged in the merger process. A list of the interviewees may be found in Appendix I.

In preparing this study, we did not contact consultants from the firms that had been engaged in guiding various aspects of the merger process. Nor did we contact representatives of the Jewish Agency for Israel (JAFI) who expressed concerns regarding the merger. Our focus was on the representatives of the three participating organizations and the JDC.

In addition to personal interviews, we mailed a questionnaire to a group of people who were either members of the advisory committee or the merger committee itself, as well as to a random selection of executives and presidents of smaller federations whose organizations were affected by the merger. Those interviewed played major and/or secondary roles in the merger process and, in a few instances, participated in prior merger discussions. Many

3

were kind enough to share correspondence, minutes, memos, and reports, some of them going back to earlier attempts at merger.

This study is about a work in progress, crafted by people bound by varying levels of interest and commitment to the organizations affected by the new agency. Even as the interviews were completed in December 2003, changes in the merged organization were still occurring. Indeed, they continue to this day. It was – and continues to be – our goal that the information collected and conclusions drawn would inform the decision-making process and the future growth of the UJC.

The study reveals a tale of unclear expectations, unshared visions, mixed motivations and multi-layered power games. But it is also a story about men and women who love the Jewish people, want to serve it, and desire to see it flourish. There are no villains. As the picture unfolds, it demonstrates the difficulties born of grafting differing organizational cultures together while seeking to merge the better or best attributes of each of these separate entities.

# ACKNOWLEDGMENTS

We each have long careers in Jewish communal service, having dedicated our lives to that calling. We were made aware of the growing discontent among many regarding the three national organizations (CJF, UJA and UIA) serving federations and Jewish concerns overseas. As the discussions leading to the establishment of the UJC unfolded and we observed the new organization and its structure emerging, we heard increasing numbers of colleagues and lay leaders voicing discontent with the outcome of what had been a long and arduous merger process. We decided it might be helpful to study the process in order to understand the motivations and procedures that led to the development of the UJC. With the encouragement of colleagues and some national leaders, we crafted a proposal for circulation. We also committed our own research funds which Hebrew Union College – Jewish Institute of Religion (HUC-JIR) provides to its faculty. Rabbi Norman J. Cohen, Provost of HUC-JIR, allowed us to move forward by promptly accepting our initial proposal. We then approached the Jerusalem Center for Public Affairs (JCPA), with which we are both affiliated, and received its endorsement.

After that, a number of friends were approached, and we are truly grateful to them for their encouragement and financial support. We could not have gone forward without them. We thank Bennett Aaron; Ben Breslauer and the Samuel and Helene Soref Foundation; Irwin Field; John Fishel and the Los Angeles Jewish Federation Council; Dr. Betsy Gidwitz; Dr. Conrad Giles; Herbert Gimelstob; Robert Goldberg; Alan Jaffe; Sidonia Lax; H. Irwin Levy; Sonny Planet; Esther Leah Ritz of blessed memory; Joel Tauber; Richard Wexler; and two friends who wish to remain anonymous.

Rabbi David Gordis, president of Boston Hebrew College and his colleague Rabbi Zachary Heller have been unusually supportive of our project in hearts, minds, and financial underwritings, which was provided through the National Center for Jewish Policy Studies (formerly the Wilstein Institute), an affiliate of the Hebrew College of Boston.

Rabbi David Ellenson, president of HUC-JIR, our friend and colleague, not only encouraged us but also provided significant underwriting for this project.

To our colleagues, Dr. Dore Gold, president; Dr. Manfred Gerstenfeld, chair of the Steering Committee and Zvi Maron, director general of the JCPA, our sincere thanks for your support and encouragement with our research.

We thank Richard Wexler for his help beyond our expectations.

Larry Rubin has played a cogent and helpful editing role.

We wish to indicate that additional donors have been approached to underwrite this research. As a result, the supporters identified above represent only a partial list of our funders.

Freddie Thomas, administrative assistant at HUC-JIR, School of Jewish Communal Service, helped us beyond measure in the production of the monograph, always exhibiting a smile and great patience.

At various stages of the project, three Jewish communal service students: Lisa Helene Helfman, MAJCS/MSW; Cassie Kirschbaum, MAJCS/MSW; and Stuart Lapowich, MAJCS/MPA were particularly helpful with their contributions.

Thanks to David Greenfield for the book cover design, and our coeditors, Nichole Morgan and Rick Dowlearn, who received an education about Jewish organizational life as they helped in the shaping and reshaping of this book.

We give special thanks to our colleague and friend, Dr. Rela Mintz Geffen, president of Baltimore Hebrew University for her very helpful critique and input.

Marla Abraham, MAJCS/MSW; our HUC colleague, was of inestimable help with perceptive inputs and critique. A special word of thanks to her.

As with previous projects, A.B. DATA, Ltd. was once again helpful in the production and distribution of our study. We particularly thank Liz Ludowissi, vice president, and others for their efforts.

We alone assume the responsibility for our conclusions and any errors of omission or commission.

We are blessed beyond measure with loving mates. At the same time, they are capable of mercilessly critiquing us and our work. For all they went through as we worked together for two years, we thank them for their love and support: Ruby Bubis and Michelle Windmueller.

Finally, we lovingly dedicate this book to our friend, colleague, and mentor Professor Daniel Elazar, z"l. He left us much too soon, but his legacy, wisdom, and insights live on.

Gerald Bubis                                        Steven Windmueller

Los Angeles, CA
March, 2005
Adar Bet, 5765

7

# METHODOLOGY

In studying the largest merger ever among nonprofit institutions and the most significant institutional transformation in modern Jewish life, we sought to uncover the core elements related to the creation of the UJC. In doing so, we examined the historical, cultural, and political factors which influenced the leadership of CJF, UJA and UIA to engage in merger discussions.

We interviewed 88 key stakeholders involved in shaping and constructing this new entity. They included federation lay and professional leaders, national CJF, UJA and UIA officers, senior executives and key figures representing the ideological and religious streams of our community. These discussions were candid, detailed and comprehensive. We were struck by the serious intent exhibited by the participants engaged in this interview process.

Our research also utilized the literature on mergers and collaborative ventures, permitting us to examine the UJC's experience against the theoretical framework and leading practices identified by others in the fields of management and business. We turned to two major sources of insight into the principles of group governance. This background provides a tool to better understand the results of our study. The first set of principles is drawn from the area of widely tested and proven theories on modern corporate management. The other is an extraction from the writings of Daniel Elazar (z"l) and Stuart Cohen on the Jewish political tradition. Drawing upon both sources, we analyzed the creation of the UJC while seeking to examine what went wrong and what went right in the merger process. Excerpts from these sources may be found in appendices II and III.

While the expertise found in the literature on mergers and acquisitions could have been utilized as a road map, neither the consultants nor participants in any serious way referred to this literature. The interviewees never mentioned such guidelines. As a result, we conclude that much of the participants' frustration with the merger process and many of the predictable pitfalls might well have been avoided if merger guidelines had been followed.

Provided below is a categorization of the 88 participants in our study:

1. thirty-three were from a group of 57 serving on the merger drafting and steering committees;
2. ten executives from among the 17 largest federations in the United States, in addition to five other professionals who direct smaller communities;
3. thirteen people serving (or having served) as CEOs of the CJF, UIA, UJA, and JDC over the past few years;
4. one former high-level sub-executive from a national agency;
5. fifteen lay people primarily identified as CJF national leaders, nine who identified with national UJA and six with UIA;  they included respondents from the religious and Zionist streams;  and,
6. eleven other observers, consultants, and former institutional participants in North America and in Israel.

**The Survey Instrument:**

The participants were asked to respond to the 11 questions:

1. *What brought about the merger of UIA, UJA, and CJF?*

2. *Were you in agreement with the idea of merger?*

3. *Did any one of the organizations involved in the merger benefit more than the others?*

4. *Would you have preferred a different model than the present one?  What would it have been?*

5. *Who were those most active in the merger process?*

6. *Did professionals play roles disproportionate to their authority?*

7.  *Did people from any particular organization seem to dominate the merger efforts?*

8.  *Were you satisfied with the final outcome?*

9.  *Did you feel the process, which produced the merged organization, a representative one?*

10. *Were there any "winners" and "losers"? Who were they?*

11. *What general lessons did you learn from the merger process?*

We synthesized the responses from our notes covering nearly 200 pages of comments. We classified the material in three different ways by:

1.  differentiating the responses of people when controlling for their primary organizational affiliation;

2.  contrasting the diversity of responses we received from executives and their lay leaders;  and,

3.  identifying various themes among the different respondents.

As a result, we provide a sense of the richness of the responses and mirror the depth of seriousness and commitment of those who were engaged in the merger process. The study seeks to place  into context a number of elements:

- the case for the merger;

- the concerns that respective parties brought to the merger discussions;

- the contours of the deliberations leading up to the development of this new entity;  and,

- finally, the conditions or expectations that were or were not met through these negotiations and the ultimate construction of the UJC.

Beyond our reporting on these findings, we have provided both an analysis of what we believe to be the salient learning points associated with the creation of the UJC and a set of recommendations which may be helpful for the UJC's own further institutional development. We believe that the considerations related to merger arrangements and collaborative efforts will be useful to other nonprofit organizations.

This document contains a rich assortment of information, focusing on the experiences associated with the framing of a new community organization and clear imperatives about transforming communities and building institutions. Five major observations are particularly relevant:

1. A new institution or a different organizational culture cannot be created if the behaviors and practices of the original organizations remain intact.

2. All institutional change is difficult and by definition creates its own unique dysfunctions. The challenge is to find ways to move strategically through the transitional process efficiently and creatively, taking as few losses as possible.

3. Before a merger process can be launched, all key stakeholders need to agree on a set of shared outcomes. Realizing that constituencies enter such a process with specific institutional agendas, they must be willing to shed or merge their goals into a set of agreed upon shared values and core objectives. Otherwise, the enterprise will be seen as structurally non-functional and ideologically flawed.

4. For a complex system to succeed, a level of institutional discipline on the part of participating organizations is required. In this particular case, the buy-in process by

necessity included more than 150 federated communities. Complicating this system's capacity to organize itself is a set of competing and challenging elements including, but not limited to, the voluntary nature of the UJC and also its international obligations, expectations, and agreements.

5. The construction of this newly "centralized" system of organizing occurred precisely during a period in which the dominant theme of American philanthropy was increased decentralization of core services and functions. Donor-directed giving, personal and institutional accountability, and entrepreneurial forms of fund development must be understood as operating in contradiction to the original intent of the emerging UJC model.

In reviewing our findings, it appears that key stakeholders can be said to have understood the merger through three perspectives relating either to motive, implementation, or goals. One segment of our interviewees described this merger model as a defensive response by the federated system designed to preserve and protect its place within the Jewish philanthropic community. Some characterized this approach as a "power play" by the large city federations, especially by their professionals, to gain control of the highly visible international component of the system. (i.e. the UJA/JAFI). In their view, the intent was to dislodge key leadership elements that had represented the core interests of both the UIA and the UJA.

The second perspective presented a very different assessment. These respondents described the process as based upon actions taken by responsible leaders with a commitment to construct an accountable and viable new model. The failure, in their minds, was more about the implementation process associated with the birthing of the UJC and less about motive or intent.

The third perspective was provided by a small number of interviewees who viewed the merger as a missed opportunity to

13

construct a truly transformational organization for the Jewish future, geared toward anticipating and responding to the issues facing Jews and Jewish life in the 21$^{st}$ century.

# INTRODUCTION

*Now Abram was rich in cattle, silver and gold.....Lot, who went with Abram, also had flocks and herds and tents, so the land could not support them staying together; for their possessions were so great that they could not remain together. And there was quarreling between the herdsmen of Abram's cattle and of Lot's cattle... Abram said to Lot: 'Let there be no strife between you and me, between my herdsmen and yours, for we are kinsmen. Is not the whole land before you? Let us separate: if you go north, I will go south; and if you go south, I will go north.' Lot looked about him and saw how well watered was the whole plain of the Jordan... so Lot chose for himself the whole plain of the Jordan (Genesis: 13: 2,5-11).*

*In the 11$^{th}$ century, Rav Gershom "...desired to establish a permanent organization of communities, such as might continue to function after his death. The code of Takkanot of R. Gershom...appears to be a....miniature constitution for such a federation...Although the empire was disunited, and travel was difficult and dangerous, while local patriotisms tended to divide the Jewish community, nevertheless the synods continued to meet even after R. Gershom could no longer lead them...Nevertheless the lack of a great leader ultimately brought about the disintegration of the federation." (Finkelstein, 1964, p. 32-35).*

In every generation, Jews have sought to build communal institutions. At times, institutions were created and shaped by divisions within the community, as in the story of Abram and Lot. At other times, as with the story of Rav Gershom in building the Rhineland confederation, leaders have constructed alliances in order to strengthen and sustain the communal enterprise.

A major debate has erupted over the creation, evolution and success of the UJC. The initiative for the merger occurred against the backdrop of major efforts, both on the corporate side and within the nonprofit sector, to establish new modalities of doing business. What follows is an exploration of the process that evolved in the creation of the UJC. Moreover, the study examines the product or outcomes by assessing earlier impressions regarding the viability and success of the enterprise. While we are not historians, we have summarized the most relevant historical events in order to put this merger into context.

We began this study with one agenda – to understand and reveal. It is the result of listening to literally hundreds of hours of interviews and reading hundreds of pages of memos, documents, and literature. Since the UJC is a work in progress, we invite those involved in directing and leading the new organization to examine, evaluate, and hopefully profit from what was shared with us.

What follows is a brief historical summary of the major national and international institutions which served the Jewish community from 1895 to1999 until the formation of the UJC. Included are two organizations that were not partners in the merger but are integral elements of the Jewish philanthropic and communal system – JDC and JAFI. They continue with the same structures as existed before the merger.

**The Merger Partners**

**Council for Jewish Federations (CJF)**

Nearly two decades before the founding of the JDC, the first federation was established in Boston. The federated model was believed to be a more efficient way to raise and allocate funds and address the needs in local Jewish communities (Bernstein, 1983; O'Brien, 1986). Almost 40 years later, a national organization was created to service the more than 200 local federations in the United States (Bernstein, 1983; O'Brien, 1986). It was originally named the "National Council of Jewish Federations and Welfare Funds". In 1932, it became known as CJF. Organizers aimed to develop standards, principles, and programming in social and communal welfare work for federations, welfare funds, and other Jewish communal service organizations in North America. The Council was primarily concerned with organizing resources to best serve the Jewish communities on the local and national levels (Bernstein, 1983; O'Brien, 1986; Schneiderman, 1933), without concentrating on issues abroad.

**United Israel Appeal (UIA)**

Created in 1925 to unify fundraising efforts of organizations including Jewish National Fund, Hadassah and Hebrew University (Stock, 1987), the "United Palestine Appeal" was dissolved in

1930. In 1936, it was revived. By 1952 it became known as the United Israel Appeal (UIA) (Stock, 1987). From its inception, the UIA served as the sole fundraising agency for the Jewish Agency for Palestine (Israel) and provided a link between the American Jewish community and Palestine (Israel). Though the UIA had the smallest operating budget of the three organizations involved in the merger, its power and land holdings in Israel allowed it to surpass both the CJF and UJA in influence within Israel.

The formation of the UIA created the need for an agency abroad to allocate funds collected in North America, and the Jewish Agency for Israel (JAFI) was established. UIA distributed the funds raised by UJA/federation campaigns to JAFI for allocation (Stock, 1987; UIA, 1997). Funds raised in North America accounted for three-fourths of JAFI's annual operating budget (Stock, 1987). Due to the funding UIA provided, its board had influence on JAFI's policies, including representation on JAFI's Board of Governors and Assembly. The composition of UIA's board changed over the years as various American Jewish organizations vied for seats in order to influence JAFI (Elazar, 1995; Stock, 1987). Beginning in 1973, the UIA annually secured and monitored grant money from the United States government for the resettlement of Jewish refugees to Israel (UIA, 1997).

**United Jewish Appeal (UJA)**

In the wake of *Kristallnacht,* when the need for more efficient fundraising to help European Jews became apparent, the UJA was formed in 1939 to unify the efforts of the United Palestine Appeal and the National Refugee Service (O'Brien, 1986; Stock, 1987). Over the following decades, the UJA grew to become the "largest voluntary philanthropy in Jewish history" (Garner, 1982, p. 9). Part of the impetus for this earlier merger came from the CJF, pressuring the organizations to unify their fundraising efforts to reduce the strain on the American Jewish community in deciding which overseas efforts to support (Raphael, 1982; Stock, 1987).

From the beginning, the UJA decided it would implement its campaigns through the local federations (Davis, 1994). This decision had a profound impact on how federations raised money. American Jews were challenged as never before to give and to increase their contributions in support of the Jewish State. This drive forever changed how federations raised funds (Davis, 1994; Karp 1981). Their combined efforts in overseas and domestic campaigns helped to bring Zionism to the American Jewish community while at the same time strengthening Jewish communities in America (Davis, 1994; Karp, 1981). After World War II, the UJA's fundraising assisted in the resettlement of Holocaust survivors both in Israel and Jewish communities worldwide (O'Brien, 1986; Raphael, 1982; Stock, 1987). As its program and stature grew, the UJA began to provide leadership development, educational programs, twinning of American and Israeli communities, and various missions to Israel (Davis, 1994).

**Affiliated Institutions**

**American Jewish Joint Distribution Committee (JDC)**

In 1914, as the shadow of World War I began to spread over Europe, the JDC was established (JDC, 2004; O'Brien, 1986). Its mission is "to serve the needs of Jews throughout the world, particularly where their lives are threatened or made more difficult" (JDC, 2004). The JDC's focus is on rescue, relief and renewal of Jewish communities around the world, to rebuild Jewish culture and religion while advancing Jewish continuity (JDC, 2004). In addition, the JDC is committed to assisting Israel in providing social services to her vulnerable communities (JDC, 2004). The JDC (also known as "the Joint") estimates that its efforts have assisted millions of Jews in 85 countries, starting in 1914 with the distribution of $50,000 to prevent Jews in Palestine and Europe from starving and continuing to this day in its response to the current economic crisis faced by the Jewish community in Argentina (JDC, 2004).

At its inception, the JDC focused on maintaining the vibrancy of worldwide Jewish communities, assisting them with rescue and relocation to Palestine only when they were at risk of destruction. That stance changed with the formation of the State of Israel when the option of relocation in the Jewish State became possible (O'Brien, 1986). The majority of the JDC's annual budget came from the UJA. Additional resources included grants from the United States government for specific programs such as the resettlement in Israel of Jewish immigrants from the Soviet Union, individual contributions, donations from foundations, international organizations and Jewish communities around the world (JDC, 2004; O'Brien, 1986).

**Jewish Agency for Israel (JAFI)**

In 1929, the World Zionist Organization (WZO) created the Jewish Agency for Palestine, which today is known as JAFI (JAFI, 1998). Before the birth of Israel, JAFI was recognized by the League of Nations as the official representative of World Jewry in forming a Jewish national home in Palestine. It was the de facto government for the territory before the State of Israel was created (Stock, 1987). After the State of Israel was recognized, JAFI remained in place to finance and organize mass immigrations and to welcome and initiate those moving to Israel (Stock, 1987). Its Board of Governors was equally composed of members of WZO and Diaspora Jews (O'Brien, 1986). JAFI's mission is dedicated to rescuing Jewish communities at risk, resettling new immigrants in Israel, encouraging and assisting those who make *aliyah*, building new settlements, bolstering Israel's economic development, providing local and worldwide Zionist education, promoting Israeli culture, enhancing Jewish unity and identity, supporting health services in Israel, and strengthening Israel as a home for all Jews. JAFI is as concerned about the well being of American Jews as it is about Israelis, since so much of its own and Israel's funding comes from America (Elazar, 1995). JAFI remains influential in both effecting Israeli politics and maintaining American-Israeli relationships (Elazar, 1995). Before 1999, JAFI was the major recipient of CJF, UIA, and UJA funds raised or transmitted for Israel. Any exceptions were locally selected programs and organizations in Israel to which a number of local federations had begun to provide direct funding.

# *ROAD TO MERGER*

The creation of the UJC did not occur in a vacuum. As noted elsewhere in this study, the idea of merging various institutions related to the national federation system and its international partners had been discussed over a number of decades. Issues of accountability and management, referenced elsewhere, were internal components that would drive the discussion around merger and consolidation.

Clearly a variety of external factors would prompt a new round of discussions in the early 1990's, leading ultimately to the formation of the United Jewish Communities by the end of the decade. Those unifying elements that had initially elevated the federation-UJA campaigns, including the birth of the State of Israel and its efforts to defend itself during three periods of conflict: 1956, '67 and '73, and the rescue and absorption of Jews from across the world were no longer seen as compelling themes driving and sustaining collective giving. As a result, not only was the federation system facing new institutional challenges from within the Jewish community for donor engagement but also as American Jews became increasingly more connected to the general philanthropic sector, other charitable groups sought to compete for their leadership and financial support. The emergence of new demographic data as referenced in the 1990 National Jewish Population Study would lead to the construction of a Jewish identity and continuity agenda that refocused communal priorities and resources.

In a dramatic powerpoint presentation entitled "On the Road to Merger," the case for merger is put before the UIA, UJA, and CJF leadership with clarity and a sense of urgency. It propounds as its goal a commitment to "provide a national structure which is effective and efficient in the delivery of valuable services and accountable to local communities." In identifying the challenges faced by federations and the national system, this document echoes many of the same characteristics or perceptions cited by our survey participants.

The consultants hired to manage the merger discussion process singled out six specific issues underlying the perceived dysfunction and institutional failure of the existing system. These included:

1. decreasing fealty to the national system;
2. intense competition between local and overseas needs;
3. dramatically declining overseas allocations;
4. no sense of connection to the national system;
5. UJA perceived as reflecting the principal of taxation without representation; adding little or no value; and,
6. CJF perceived as incompetent in most departments.

These observations might be measured against a series of questions proposed by Yankey, Wester and Campbell (1998) for non-profit agencies to consider when contemplating the option of merger or consolidation:

1. What resources does the agency lack; how important are these resources; and where might the agency secure them?

2. What will be required to make the agency more competitive in the future and what are the "strategic options"?

3. How do key stakeholders and funders view the organization and its credibility, and what "characteristics" should be identified in a merger partner who might increase its credibility and legitimacy with stakeholders and funders?

4. What are the "potential changes in community values" that may impact the agency, and what might the community ask of the agency to meet these changes in values?

5. In what functional areas are the agency least efficient, and what characteristics should be identified in a merger partner to increase its efficiency?

From the consultants' observations as well as the queries derived from the literature, we deduced that the factors driving the merger process were directed toward:

1. promoting efficiencies within a new national organization;
2. protecting and advancing the overseas-Jewish Agency agenda; and,
3. serving the interests of local federations.

A richer discussion of these issues is provided elsewhere in this book.

## UIA

From a UIA perspective, the responses of both professionals and volunteers ranged from benign to bitter (with the majority by far tilting toward the latter). One long time participant noted that the first moves toward merger began in 1948 when "Ben Gurion separated money without Jews and Jews without money," thus first stripping UIA and the Zionists of their political power.

### Misunderstanding the Uniqueness of the UIA:

As noted, few people understood the unique role of UIA. This complaint was often accompanied by the observation that UIA's budget was less than one-tenth the budget of both the UJA and CJF. UIA was the designated oversight instrument for United States government funds that go to Israel through UJA. Similarly, it is the owner of enormous assets in Israel, the funnel through which tens of millions of dollars flow annually. Its unique role has often not been appreciated or understood. In fact, during early merger discussions the inclusion of the UIA was not even on the table

Many respondents pointed out that the UIA structure is widely representative of American Jewish life. Their advocates commented that only within the UIA were the religious streams, Zionist groups, and federations at the same table. Because it is not confined to the federation world, this structure, they would argue, came closest to replicating the European and Israeli models of board representation. Moreover, UIA was the instrument through which representatives were chosen to participate in the Jewish Agency for Israel. It is fair to say that UIA leaders saw their institution as performing a unique function on behalf of American Jewry.

As the merger proceeded, most UIA respondents felt they were watching a "battle of the titans." Many of their representatives viewed the UIA as "being swept into the merger." In the end, they believed that their agency was "acquired" by the merger process; it did not become a partner with the UJA and CJF.

The UIA participants were especially critical of the CJF professional and lay leaders who, they felt, had little understanding or appreciation of the unique nexus UIA provided between American Jewry and Israel. They voiced great disappointment, and, at times, anger at the perceived insensitivity and ignorance rampant among the professional and lay leadership. A former executive director noted how the federations had not realized how much under-utilized power American Jewry had at JAFI through their UIA representatives. One of the most venerable lay leaders in America, who was not primarily affiliated with the UIA, stated, "Nothing hurts as much as the disappearance of UIA as a truly independent agency."

Few outside of the UIA grasped the special oversight function performed by the agency. This function served to assure the American government that the funds sent to Israel through UJA and on to the Jewish Agency were spent in compliance with American nonprofit regulations and laws. It also did not seem to be well known among Jewish leaders, except to those who were active at the highest levels, that the UIA has been designated by the United States government to monitor the funds raised through local federations which are transferred to JAFI for expenditure in Israel. It was charged with assuring the government that the funds are used for nonpolitical purposes. The U.S. State Department also transferred millions of dollars annually through the UIA for use by JAFI in resettling immigrants from the Former Soviet Union. Initially, the amount was $80 million annually. In recent years, because of the decreasing flow of immigrants, the annual amount was reduced to $60 million.

In assessing the new UJC structure, most UIA respondents believed that large cities were over-represented, and the voice and power of intermediate and small cities were diminished. Another result of the restructuring was the "disenfranchisement" of many Jewish organizations, as one person asserted. UIA represented the broadest spectrum of Jews in America, it was said. Almost everyone pointed out that when the merger was effectuated, it made the UJC the instrument only of the federations. "The absence of religious and Zionists streams on the new board was seen as a great loss in creating opportunities for dialogue and discussion of differences on various issues and concerns," noted one participant.

By contrast, the concerns of UIA leaders did not seem to have significant credence with UJA leadership. Most of them described UIA's functions as "blurred," "no longer needed," "unclear" and of little or less importance. Many UIA participants found it ironic that while the names of CJF and UJA disappeared for legal reasons, the UIA's remained (for a five year period) within the new organization, despite the fact that its functions and responsibilities were vastly reduced.

**Assessing How the JDC Escaped Consideration:**

A number of UIA participants noted how the JDC had excused itself from the merger process. While JDC was another beneficiary of overseas allocations through UJA (the other being JAFI), "somehow, with the entire merger talk calling for efficiency in this whole process, no one ever shined a spotlight on JDC," a respondent pointed out. The Joint had come through this process "under the radar," as described by one interviewee. By remaining outside of the merger process, JDC escaped the scrutiny that was directed toward the participating agencies.

# UJA

## The Loss of the Jewish Brand Name:

The decision to discard the highly identifiable UJA label was seen by most UJA respondents as a major disaster. The often-voiced desire for efficiency and effectiveness, along with the need for more accountability in budgetary matters, were seen as legitimate. But the merger also marked a desire by federation leaders, it was felt, to weaken and eliminate UJA as an identifiable entity. As one respondent put it, "The greatest brand name Jews had has been destroyed in the process. While the merger's goal was unifying, the result is splintering, drunk and disorderly by comparison with the past." This decision to discard the UJA name was described by many interviewees as a major institutional mistake.

Philanthropic "brand names," similar to corporate product recognition, hold special market value in our society. Hall (2004) states, "If the estimates are accurate, charity brands are worth a lot. United Way of America's brand has a value of $34.7 billion, according to Interbrand; enough to fall just behind the top four multinational companies on a ranking of corporate brands issued last month by a consulting company and Business Week. If charities were include in the ranking, United Way would be ranked after Coca-Cola, Microsoft, IBM, and GE and just ahead of Walt Disney" (Chronicle of Philanthropy, August 5, 2004). The interest in estimating the worth of a nonprofit brand marks a new phase in the growing sophistication of marketing efforts under way at the nation's charities. Since the late 1990s, many nonprofit groups have borrowed the techniques of the corporate sector and emphasized their 'brand' in an array of ways. "The experts also analyze a charity's name recognition, its stability, geographical reach, and ability to appeal to diverse audiences." Large charities, according to Hall, "could reap many benefits by undertaking brand evaluations . . ."

We can only conclude that this loss of brand name was a grave error.

**Establishing a Base Line for Overseas Dollars:**

In reviewing the responses of the UJA interviewees in general, it became apparent that they were often reluctant participants in the merger process. In all instances, however, they were seeking to safeguard the most salient roles and functions of the UJA, believing that Jewish life benefited from a voice solely devoted to Israel and other overseas needs.

Many UJA leaders feared a further plummeting of resources for overseas causes. Thus, a number of people entered into the merger to protect allocations to Israel and other international Jewish concerns. They saw merger as the only way to stem the hemorrhaging of dollars that had been raised in the name of overseas needs but had been diverted to meet pressing domestic priorities.

This passion around overseas needs has diminished since the merger. As one person put it, "The importance of that UJA voice is gone, enveloped in a gibberish sounding name – ONAD [the UJC's Overseas Needs Assessment and Distribution Committee]." One respondent reasoned that a merger that would have insured a guaranteed sum of money annually might have been an acceptable outcome. A proposal along these lines explained his support for the merger. His reasoning echoed the feelings of many UJA respondents. According to UJC officials, because of the agreement made in the merger discussion, the rapid descent in the proportion of dollars sent overseas has been markedly contained. Thus, it appears that the UJA leaders' fallback position was validated.

Upon reflection, the failure of earlier merger discussions in the eighties was thought to have resulted in weakening the position of the UJA. A corresponding outcome, in the minds of many UJA supporters, was that "Israel was the loser in this process." Several observers also suggested that the failure of JAFI's leadership to defend the UJA in the merger negotiations contributed ultimately to its weakening. Several individuals commented as well that the merger would not have taken place had UJA leadership been stronger.

## CJF AND FEDERATION LEADERS

Four past chairpersons of the CJF were among the many federation leaders interviewed for this study. In addition, we had occasion to interview a past UJC chair. These leaders described the three most important goals of those most favoring the merger: to effectuate dollar savings; to insure federation control over the allocation of funds; and to achieve more transparency regarding the expenditure of dollars overseas.

Most of the former chairs did not agree with the initial stated premises for the merger. They believed in varying degrees that the professionals of the most powerful federations desired to reconstruct the existing system and were supported in this effort by their respective lay leaders. When looking at the outcome, all five perceived a high level of discontent among local and national leaders. They described the criticism of the UJC as ranging from lukewarm to vociferous.

One of the five feared there would be a lack of equity in the distribution of dollars overseas and locally. This individual strongly believed that the name "UJA" should not have been lost, feeling it represented a great "brand name." He had favored making the UJA a subsidiary organization to the newly-merged organization. This would have kept UJA's name intact. His idea is modeled after the local pattern, where UJA or United Jewish Fund (UJF) is part of some federations but with no independent legal status.

30

In contrast to the dire predictions of some UJA participants, two of the past chairs feared that UJA's leadership would "take over" the system and/or not ever allow CJF's leadership and staff to "control" the newly-merged organization.

**Other Federation Voices:**

CJF and other federation leadership provided us with a rich body of responses. This group included six CJF board members and 15 local federation executives. Almost all of the respondents mentioned that their support for the merger process was motivated by a desire for greater efficiency in the utilization of funds on the national level. A small number believed that the UIA was no longer relevant as a separate instrument of the Jewish people but acknowledged that the funds managed by that agency were seen as an important consideration in the merger process. They wanted transparency in the management of expenditures and distribution of resources coupled with the understanding that dollars raised locally should be monitored by a community-based system. This seemed to explain the mantra "we own the system," which evolved among local and federation leaders as a result of the merger. To a majority of these respondents this also meant that the functions heretofore provided by the UJA would now be absorbed into the federation system. There were no differences on this point between lay leaders and federation executives.

Concerns were raised regarding control of dollars spent overseas, especially those funds within the purview of JAFI. This group generally observed that the system as it had existed allowed UIA leadership too much latitude in selecting American representatives to JAFI's Board of Governors. In the opinion of some federation leaders, the Jewish Agency representatives were out of touch with the growing demand for more resources to be expended locally.

Similarly, several federation leaders believed that the UJA represented a "top down" system of management in directing its

Israel operations and in controlling its resources. According to some of those we interviewed, this may explain why local federations desired control over the UJA rather than simply merging as equals. The resultant new structure attempted to lower UJA's power by establishing the overseas pillar (ONAD) as a substitute.

One respondent reported that as a result of the "insensitive response" of UJA and UIA leadership to the communities' description of pressing communal needs, some large city federations had begun to explore the idea of creating an independent group of federations that would operate outside of the three national organizations. In this context, even the CJF was viewed as no longer meeting satisfactorily the needs of these communities.

In analyzing the process, one leader commented as follows: "Too little attention was being given to cultivating and involving lay leaders. When professionals run ahead of their lay leaders, disaster results." This same individual noted, "Not all leaders involved in the merger or post-merger process really understood the system. Some had a private agenda beyond what the merger suggested or provided."

Many federation professionals felt that they and their colleagues on the local level gained a great deal of power over the new organization, either directly or indirectly. Some saw several of their colleagues as tending to dominate the merger process. Most often, if they held this view, it was not a pejorative comment but an acknowledgement that lay leadership trusted them and counted on their knowing more and thus naturally playing a more active role.

## THE OBSERVERS

The last group of respondents that we analyzed includes representatives of the JDC and an assortment of "players" who held no official positions at the time in any of the organizations that were engaged in merger.

One of the observers began his comments by declaring with some vigor that the merger "took the extraordinary and made it ordinary. God's work is being turned into a business reengineering process. Passion and vision were removed from the work of the Jewish people, especially by eliminating UJA. Consultants were not needed. They helped to move the whole national system into a business model, while destroying the uniqueness of Jewish funding. Consequently, what had begun as a legitimate move toward increasing efficiency and effectiveness of these national organizations failed to materialize. The consultants, who really knew little about Jewish life, were unable to access or appreciate these organizational cultures. The end result was leaders, both professional and lay, running from the system, driven by the failure of the consultants to appreciate the Jewish nuance." The overemphasis of this approach, in the opinion of this observer, did not fit into what he called "the world or persuasion, love and passion [for causes.]"

According to this respondent, the driving force was the professionals, not the lay leaders. He pointed out that one of the major lay leaders had written a vitriolic book about the whole process. While he questioned the inclusion of judgments of people by name, he nonetheless agreed that the manuscript's feeling tones reflected the realities experienced by many of his lay friends.

This commentator would have preferred the creation of two organizations, one geared to overseas priorities and national programs, with the second focusing on local needs and concerns. He believes that much-needed coordination and cooperation would

33

have taken place functionally, as was the case in the past. (UIA would still be eliminated in his model).

In assessing the politics of merger, he noted that motives and passions were uneven. Some desired power, some guarded turf, and some were too conciliatory, not appreciating the full implications of the proposed new organizations. The aforementioned "mantra" of federation ownership came to be the dominant focus, especially among the executives, because of the power of local federations,. National leaders recognized that the power of the purse rested with the communities. Finally, this observer expressed the view that there was too much "process and representativeness," around the table. In his view, a smaller group could have achieved a better outcome.

Other observers concluded that at times professionals overstepped their boundaries, some occasionally pushing lay leaders onto the defensive, which resulted in a bad process and a bad product. The end result, as one put it, was a process that attained the "lowest common denominator in search of the highest common standard." In the name of consensus, sharp differences in organizational cultures and styles were never adequately addressed. One respondent asked what might have happened if the consultants had said for example, "UJA as a group raises the most dollars and has the best leaders. It should be the lead organization in the merger."

The major lesson learned is that business principles cannot be applied in their totality to the not for profit world. No framework was built into the planning that would have permitted stakeholders to acknowledge their institutional loyalties. Hence, defensiveness prevailed. The result, therefore, proved unsatisfactory to many.

Another observer directed many of his comments to the history of prior attempts to merge two or more of the organizations and supplied us much treasure from of his private papers, organizational minutes and documents. He reminded us that the present merger was the last of many attempts to bring the organizations together beginning in 1948.

According to this source, a number of core factors shaped the inter-organizational dynamics, including the power (or lack thereof) of various personalities over the decade; the differences in the organizational cultures, especially between the UJA, JDC and CJF; and the ebb and flow of various historical events. The shift in priorities and relative importance of CJF and UJA changed markedly in the 1980's, in this observer's opinion, when UJA professional leadership was drawn for the first time from the ranks of federation executives.

This observer concluded that the introduction of the practice of engaging federation executives (which became the norm) marked the beginning of what he perceived as the movement toward merger. In later years, a number of staff and lay people began to leave UJA as they perceived a tonal shift among professionals undermining the passion for a separate, independent organization. The events also accelerated the tensions between lay leaders and staff within that system.

This observer drew no conclusion as to the intentions or motivations of those involved in the abrasive push-pull of merger. He thought that a more coordinated and cooperative approach should have become the standard for the process. As a result of the tense climate that emerged, the "passion light was dimmed, if not extinguished." The documents he supplied (many of them confidential at the time) confirmed the complications, resistances, resentments and general low level of trust which often existed between all the major players.

The need, according to another observer, to create a merger was manifest. UJA "had become a general without an army and CJF had an army without a general." In this person's opinion, the notion of federation "ownership" had doomed the new organization to function in the narrowest of terms. The visionary thinking, which should have animated the merger process, failed to occur. This respondent believed an opportunity was missed to create some type of bicameral approach to governance along British parliamentary lines. Some sort of "House of Lords" would have provided a structure for significant and meaningful involvement of the so-called mega-givers in a role never before imagined in Jewish life. Issues of great matter and moment could have engaged this important leadership cadre and in the process brought them closer to the new communal infrastructure. The result would have been the sharing of their wisdom and wealth. The "House of Commons" would have engaged those most involved in the day-to-day concerns of Jewish life and could have been developed with a specific focus and commitment to broad representation.

No one seemed to appreciate that this whole enterprise was the largest reorganization attempted in the 20th century by any nonprofit organization. As the outlines of the UJC began to emerge, this observer believed that the Financial Resources Development (FRD) pillar was too narrowly conceived. He saw this as emblematic of a larger issue where, in his opinion, most participants hoped the merger would serve specific institutional needs and priorities rather than trying to evolve a new organization which could address global concerns. At the same time, this individual represented one of the few participants to comment on the "geographic issues" – the relative indifference of easterners, for example, to the question of proportionately involving people from the West.

He also offered some revolutionary ideas pertaining to ONAD. He called for this structure to be independent with authority to monitor overseas organizations through its planning and allocation process. He would have kept the philanthropic pillar as a funnel of interest. It was his opinion that this would have been a way to continue to engage the interest and commitment of mega-givers. In his view, the new UJC board could have the power to review, modify, and ultimately ratify ONAD's activities. More of those committed to UJA, according to this person, would have remained involved within the system.

A part of his model, which he would have housed separately, would have been geared primarily to serving local federations. There should have also been a pillar for constituent services and various departments devoted to human development. These would have included volunteer and professional training and financial services (for both fundraising and fiscal management) along with the present Jewish Renaissance and Renewal pillar.

He pointed out that a number of key UIA and UJA people were excluded from the merger process. In this regard, he concluded that some federation executives had exceeded their authority and thereby compromised their ability to perform a functional and helpful role in the process. Their motivation, he asserted, was to keep the system together while guaranteeing that its control would be placed in local federation hands. In many instances, he perceived this intention to control the UJA as "pay back" for past browbeating by UJA leaders, both professional and lay.

Yet another observer was more upbeat. He put his comments in a global context, pointing out that the United States is the best-organized Jewish community throughout the Diaspora. Whatever evolved as a result of the merger, the UJC was in no danger of collapsing. Indeed, its overall vitality has reached undreamed of heights.

This observer understood the heart of the merger process to be a fight over the allocation of resources – local requirements versus overseas needs. To him, the merger discussions began with a consensus, namely, that the UIA was superfluous, the UJA had financially peaked, and the CJF had proven itself ineffective. At the same time, this individual had some definite views on professionals and their performance. Local federations are led by "mandarins," he said, some more effectively than others. Federation and national professionals often assumed they could "ride out" their lay leaders whose terms of service would end. In his view, the best executives rejected that strategy. Rather, they sought to engage and educate their leaders to the benefits of the newly-created system where, he lamented, too little interactive education of this kind was taking place.

He generally judged the UJA as having the strongest core of leaders. But regardless of the organization's strong lay leaders, professionals often end up playing the dominant roles, even if that had not been the initial intention.

He saw the federation system as highly dependent upon the Jewish Agency. "JAFI still represents the closest thing to a Jewish parliament for Jews worldwide," he concluded. Federations tend to view the Agency as another social service agency and have not learned how to work within it in order to maximize the benefits to their communities. JAFI was expected to function within ONAD, but, from his perspective, had not done an effective job in adjusting to this new institutional reality. By contrast, he said, the JDC had adapted swiftly and adroitly to the new world created by the merger.

In reflecting on the merger process itself, he believed it was a representative one with the best possible result given all the political realities. As to who "lost," he thought it was obvious that the UIA had suffered the gravest defeat, while both the UJA and CJF lost their individuality. The uniqueness of some of their respective services was also lost in the process. The loss of UJA as a brand name was a huge one, "the best known organization in America," he said.

Given the reality of what exists as a result of the merger, he strongly hoped that the UJC will provide ways of becoming an open forum to discuss some of American Jewry's vexing problems and challenges such as "who is a Jew," the propriety and place of public funding for sectarian agencies, recruitment, training, and retention of both lay and professional leaders. He believed there was a special need for the UJC to train people to become tomorrow's major cities executives. He also hoped the UJC would become a more effective advocate for overseas funding. In his judgment, ONAD had yet to fulfill its stated intention to be an effective instrument to advocate for and protect overseas concerns.

He expressed concern that some of the larger issues facing Jewish life worldwide were given little or no consideration by American Jews (and thus by the UJC.) These issues were beyond philanthropy but needed focused attention, he said. He identified three major concerns. The first was the very survival of the State of Israel as a result of the contending visions and fissures within Israel itself. Can Israel survive as a Jewish, democratic, Zionist country? Israel is increasingly divided by the lack of consensus as to how the State is to achieve these goals and indeed survive. The second was his concern as to how 13 million Jews would fare in a world with well over one billion Muslims, with its undercurrent of Islamic fanaticism. The need to effectuate strategies for Israel and for all World Jewry is urgent. The third area was the rising tide of anti-Semitism coupled with the need to differentiate between anti-Semites and those who love Israel and honestly criticize the government of Israel because of its actions in the current intifada. At the same, he believes too few Jewish leaders appreciated the context for the West Bank Palestinians' action. He decried their use of suicide bombers but believes Jewish leaders had not helped themselves by failing to learn more about the "enemy." He concluded that the "time bomb" of Israeli Arabs would explode because of Israel's long held negative attitudes toward them, coupled with inadequate and discriminatory actions. This had resulted in not providing needed services for all Israeli citizens, especially Israeli Arabs.

These larger questions are beyond philanthropy but in need of public discourse. He was not in favor of any attempts to move toward a "Kehilla-like" structure. Rather he favored some kind of loose national structure that would encourage varieties of creative expression, including competition where needed and cooperation when possible. While he offered no specific blueprint, he believes the UJC has the possibility of fulfilling that role.

In the merger process itself, tensions between the negotiators ran high at times. The fears and expectations of the three organizational cultures and their respective leadership structures slowed the merger process itself. One past chair noted that when "you do a deal" in business (i.e., merge companies), the longer the process "the more angst, more differences emerge, professional vendettas arise, anguish and emotions take over on all sides and that is what happened over the seven year [merger] process." He could not believe the enmity that arose at times. As a result, he saw all these elements come to life in the merger discussions.

In the opinion of a number of lay leaders, much of this was caused by the excessive roles played by some federation professionals. As a consequence, a number of long time lay leaders withdrew from involvement in the new UJC structure. Some of them believed they were eased out of significant roles. Even as some lay leaders complained about "excessive" involvement of professionals, a number of former chairs bemoaned the lack of ongoing professional leadership on the national level. At this critical juncture in the development of the new entity, they felt that a professional leadership vacuum had resulted.

In retrospect, this respondent believed the merger was effectuated for the wrong reasons: efficiency, transportation, saving overhead and local control. The question of what will be best for the American Jewish community was never addressed. The result, in this person's opinion, was a group of well meaning people who got sidetracked. (Two other respondents raised regrets as to their own role in the process, feeling, as one put it, they were "too passive.")

The respondent further believed that UJA leaders were never realistic in acknowledging the importance of changing priorities on the local level. They never addressed how these needs could be funded, given the recent history of flat campaigns. UJA participants, he believed, minimized the impact of the growing demand for dollars for Jewish education and Jewish identity enhancement programs and the growing number of Jewish elderly and poor.

The preponderant view of the observers was that a clear dominance of the process was established by CJF and federation leaders. More so than the past chairs who were interviewed, the observers tended to share many negative perceptions regarding both the merger process and its ultimate outcome – the UJC itself.

# INCORPORATING THE DIVERSITY OF RESPONSES: PROFESSIONALS AND LAY LEADERSHIP

## Professionals

### Assessing the Process – Federation Professionals

One federation professional listed four reasons that motivated his support for a merger:

1. The existing allocations system for international purposes under UJA's umbrella simply made no sense.

2. Allocations for overseas purposes (JAFI and JDC) "were hemorrhaging" so a new distribution system was required in order to meet overseas obligations in a responsible way.

3. The method of allocating resources needed rationalizing and a "needs-based" approach, as a substitute for "back room dealings."

4. Finally, a new unified national system would be required if the problems and challenges confronting the Jewish people were to be responsibly and adequately addressed.

This professional believed that the UIA was a "waste of time," no longer clear regarding its focus and functions. As a result, it should not remain the funnel through which American Jewish leaders were chosen members of the Board of Governors of JAFI.

This director thought the merger got "off to a bad start. Those who believed it would make for better fund raising, a better voice for American Jewry, and more responsibility responding to overseas needs have not seen it happen." He felt in retrospective that he "had been naive. . . .I bought into the notion that federations would do the right thing for the Jewish people by doing the best for the collectivity." Instead, he saw a drive among his colleagues and others "to own the system." The end result produced "a lot of owners" who in fact never acted as [a unified management] but rather continued to see the whole outcome as a 'we-they' situation." No one was ready for reform, he concluded, including his own lay leaders.

In this participant's opinion, most of those involved were fearful of the future. In his mind "any federation's potentiality and strength comes from its own engagement with the great issues, events, and concerns facing Jews. If not, a federation is just another charity and not the primary entity it could and should be in Jewish life today."

The majority of his colleagues mentioned efficiency and effectiveness as the primary reason for the merger. A number of them referred to "the seamless way local and overseas needs were handled locally as compared to the national structures." Thus, there was wide concurrence, as expressed by one director, on the need to rationalize "a national structure, which could comprehensively respond to changing needs." There was a desire to redesign the old network of overlapping functions and players with a new "more representative system." A number focused their reasoning on the need to control the UJA. One professional framed the merger process as being "driven" by the desire of many of his colleagues to gain control over "a unified national apparatus."

Another professional expressed the belief that he was not sure that UJA and UIA leaders were aware of the level of dissatisfaction with their agencies. He pointed out that, during his time in the field, many visions for a more comprehensive approach to addressing changing needs had been blocked by major UJA and UIA players. This moment in history, although brought about by often-unshared motivations, made the process for merger finally possible, he said.

Though nuanced in their responses, all the federation directors favored the merger. The majority of key federation directors thought they and their colleagues were most active in the merger discussions. Some colleagues were criticized for being too active. Others believed their colleagues were appropriately helpful to lay leaders in moving the process along.

Two professionals were critical of the role of the consulting companies. One said that they raised expectations too high, and they were insufficiently appreciative of the distinctive cultures of the national organizations. These individuals believed that there was an over-emphasis by the consultants on the model of a "trade association" among federations, which ultimately lowered the bar on considering other creative responses in constructing a new organization.

Ironically, another executive commented that inefficiencies and inadequacies on the national level were precisely the result of the CJF being primarily a "trade organization," narrowly focused and functioning accordingly. This respondent wanted a new organization, one that would not be seen as a trade association but rather would serve as a magnet for attracting mega-givers and their financial clout in responding to the multiplicity of challenges facing Jewish life. He believed strongly that a merger would result in a number of outcomes: cost reductions, greater communal support for overseas needs, and the creation of an open system for institutional priority setting.

The issue of board representation was tied to the differing visions of the emerging UJC. Some executives believed that a new national board structure should include representatives of the synagogue movements, thus becoming a more representative body. They argued that such a structure would serve federations overarching goals. Other directors disagreed, saying the organization should continue to see itself as a representative body for the federations, while keeping synagogue representatives within the renewal and renaissance pillar.

One director believed the lack of rabbis and synagogue or movement-based lay leadership on the new board is an error. He observed, "the action lies elsewhere," referring to the development and growth of such organizations as Partnership for Excellence in Jewish Education (PEJE), Heart Share, and the New Israel Fund (NIF). At the very least, he said, more coordinated relations could and should be developed with these and other such bodies.

Another federation director favored the decision to keep rabbinic and lay representatives from the religious streams off the board. His logic was that they had no primary loyalty to the federations and that the UJC had been shaped into the federations' national body. Nevertheless, this respondent agreed with his colleague that a mistake had been made in relegating both the religious and Zionist streams to an inconsequential role within the new structure. This decision demonstrated the continuing tug of war as to whether the UJC was an organization for the Jewish people or an organization for Jewish federations. If it were to function largely as a federation "trade association," he said, calling it the "United Jewish Federations of North America" might have resolved some of the ambiguity.

Yet a number of federation directors actively resisted the "trade association" label. A few of the executives wanted to see the UJC address the "mega-issues" facing the Jewish community but recognized that this could only happen when significantly increased fund raising took place. (However, there was no consensus among the executives as to what the mega-issue priorities were so that they might be addressed in a coherent and coordinated manner.) In a dysfunctional national system, one executive observed, there is no ability to address national issues. Invariably, in his opinion, price tags were put on everything. He believed major issues, which had no monetary implications in and of themselves, were never addressed. The convening role of the UJC needed more emphasis, he suggested. In his judgment, there can never be a central address for Jewish life in America, but the UJC could nevertheless act as a major convener.

Paradoxically, taking the price tag off large issues may attract more engagement and ultimately more resources. This same executive noted, "Without large donors, no large ideas can be fulfilled." As a convener, he pointed out, the UJC could provide a venue and structure for mega-givers to connect with the community around the major issues facing Jewish life. He further proposed having the UJC refocus its mission statement; establish incubators by funding experimental programs dealing with complex issues in order to provide models for implementation in the communities; consult with schools of Jewish communal service about the caliber of their students and the effectiveness of their curricula; interview the schools' graduates to assess the impact that they as professionals have made on shaping the field; and hire a national consultant to assess the professional needs of the field and recommend the services needed for recruiting, funding, and developing more appropriate curriculums for the field of Jewish communal work.

The breadth of such proposals implies the degree of dissatisfaction that a number of federations executives felt regarding progress to date. The merger, in one director's eyes, had not added anything helpful to Jewish life because there was little trust or understanding of the new venture on the local level. He went on to criticize the lack of openness in the system, lamenting the absence of both mega-givers and the creative community. He pointed out that at a time when synagogues and federations were coming together locally as never before, the new national structure of the UJC had "missed the boat" in not reflecting that reality.

Unhappiness was reflected in suggestions to either turn back the clock or strike off in an entirely different direction. The major change in leadership on the local level had further complicated the focusing and refining of the merger process. As a result of these uncertainties, a number of people would prefer dismantling the UJC and returning to the prior arrangement of three different organizations. Their wishes, while unreal, affect their commitment to helping the UJC succeed.

Perhaps more salient was the suggestion by several professionals that a confederation of large federations, separate from a similar grouping of small federations, be created. This would recognize the markedly diverse needs and interests of federations, as referenced by such standards as the size of the community and the campaign status. A few believed that any new configuration would need to retain the UJA's name, describing it as the "best brand and most well-known name in America."

In contrast to the observers who felt the merger process dragged on much too long, some professionals believed that it had proceeded too quickly. This resulted in local federations not fully understanding what the merged organizations intended to accomplish other than so-called federation "ownership" of the new structure. Some voiced caution about making final judgments about the UJC so early in the merger process. They saw Jewish life as changing so fast that there has been insufficient time, as one put it, "for the care and feeding of the newly-created organization."

Another director was more satisfied and optimistic than most regarding the UJC while still voicing concerns. He saw "the glass as half-full, a work in progress, needing nourishment, encouragement and further shaping for future development." In his opinion, the major concerns were operational – e.g., the loss of UJA's name – which could be easily corrected.

The most important issue for this executive director was to develop a consensus on the part of the federated system as to how this new organization should move forward. The core principles underlying the case for merger need to be regularly reviewed and their implementation monitored. While cost is always a factor, he said, the quality and deployment of staff must be seen as a paramount ingredient in the success of this venture. Support for experimentation must be seen as critical in judging the success of the UJC.

In his opinion, the "jury is still out" as to whether or not the UJC can deal with these concerns. One of the unsolved questions was what would or could be binding on local communities as a requirement for membership in the UJC. Another colleague observed that there was an insufficient number of lay people involved at the national level. Similarly, to more and more of his colleagues, the ONAD pillar "was a disaster" in the sense that the passion and drive of the UJA had been lost, and its current mission lacked sufficient clarity. Without resolution of these issues, he said, no coherence would be possible on the national level. At the time of these interviews (late in 2003), none of these issues had been resolved; no true merger of the various organizational cultures had taken place. The notion of the pillars had not yet produced the desired integrative results but rather appeared to have separated CJF-oriented people from UJA- identified participants.

Three final observations. We would not have been surprised if a significant number of executives discussed the need for more local control to assure that local needs remained the highest priority. Rather, our interviews highlighted the commitment most had to finding new ways of maintaining or increasing support for overseas needs. While there were differences on how best to do this, (e.g., through a donor – designated giving program funneling money away from JAFI or finding new funding sources), their profound concern for Israel was palpable.

Secondly, a significant number of federation professionals lamented the loss of knowledgeable and engaged national leaders but also noted the crisis in recruiting, developing, and retaining the requisite number and quality of young leaders that the new system would require. As one put it, the original organizations were perpetuated by engaging the same people in a new disguise. What is required, he suggested, was serious contemplation of a radical change in the type of lay leaders and professionals needed.

Lastly, the responses of federation executives from smaller cities dovetailed with the perceptions and analyses of their colleagues from larger communities. However, comparing the responses of executives in general to their lay counterparts provided a more striking difference than was the case when comparing UIA and UJA executives with their respective lay leaders.

**Assessing the Process – National Agency Executives**

We analyzed the responses of the CJF/UJA executive pool in order to identify the degree to which there was agreement or disagreement in their assessments. As might be expected, by virtue of their positions, answers were filled with nuances and shaded with grays rather than absolutes. Those executives favoring the merger reasoned that a more disciplined and predictable collectivity of federations would produce more dollars for Israel. As "owners the system," they thought, federations would become more conscious of Israel's needs. The idea of "collective responsibility" became an important tool to effectuate the twin goals of generating more dollars for Israel and also achieving a more balanced representation on JAFI's Board of Governors. As one executive put it, the national system had created a "disconnect" by not being responsive to local – i.e., federation – donors. The leadership of UIA blocked discussions between givers and spenders, and both UIA and UJA blocked systematic ways of getting the desired overseas input and output.

Joining a number of other participants from all sectors of the study, one national executive opted for a new structure of partnerships or alliances. He reasoned that efficiencies could have been effectuated with all three groups sharing space and what he called "backroom faculties" (office staff, technical support, joint insurance, supplies, etc.) plus an opportunity for joint ventures in certain services. This approach would have, in his opinion, provided opportunities for better services through coordination and cooperation while maintaining the strengths of each respective organization. More people would have stayed involved. This executive obviously did not favor the merger as such.

Contrary to the criticisms of lay and professional leaders in many federations, the majority of national agency executives believed that the UJA was transparent in both its governance process and management of resources. JDC was referenced by one executive as a model of effectiveness, efficiency, and focus as compared to all the other organizations involved in the merger.

Two executives felt the merger came about out of necessity. The status quo was totally inadequate and radical action was necessary to correct the deficiencies in the national system. One of these executive felt that "there was a necessary and desirable creative tension" among the three national organizations. In his view, the merger might have blunted institutional differences even if it failed to generate the efficiencies that would truly save money.

Most of the respondents agreed that pressure from local lay and professional leaders, coupled with the input of a significant group of national lay leaders, brought about the impetus for merging the three organizations.

In summary, the national executives, all past or present CJF and UJA CEOs, agreed on a number of issues but were not unanimous in all of their perceptions or conclusions. All of them saw the primary reasons for the merger as emanating from federation leadership, both on the local and national level, who were dissatisfied with the perceived lack of transparency in the UJA and/or JAFI operations.

While most CJF and UJA executives initially favored the merger, no one was satisfied with the newly formed UJC, some even seeing it as a totally unsatisfactory outcome. Most were quite pessimistic about its future unless radical changes took place. They believed that their local federation colleagues were vociferous in demanding that a federation CEO be brought in to fill the new national position. After that principle was accepted, the local CEOs became "carping critics for the most part," to quote one national executive, and gave insufficient support and cooperation to their former colleagues.

There was not total agreement on who benefited the most from the merger. Some believed that JDC was the big winner because it had been left out of the merger. This gave the Joint more autonomy to raise money separately while being funded as part of the allocations process of the federation system.

Most of the national executives thought that their federation colleagues dominated the merger process and had gained control over the new organization, either directly or indirectly. The CEOs also asserted that a number of their colleagues had varying private or personal agendas. There were clear exceptions, as one federation director and one national CEO were specifically lauded for their statesmanlike and professional approach to the merger process.

Most often, if a national executive felt that a federation professional dominated the discussions, it was not a pejorative comment. It was instead recognition that lay leadership trusted their professionals, counted on their wisdom, and consequently relied on them to play a more active role.

On a broader level, however, no organizations were seen as dominating, though a few individuals thought that a couple of cities provided a disproportionate number of people (professional and lay) who tended to be more active than people from other cities.

## Lay Leadership

### Lay Leaders Assess the Professionals

Most of the lay leaders who were interviewed expressed general satisfaction about the merger process. However, their responses became more deliberative and expansive when discussing the role of the professionals. Since lay-professional relations have surfaced as an integral part of this study, we believe it is important to report the perceptions of the involved lay leaders and examine some of the consequences.

The issue of lay-professional relations has long been on the communal agenda. In fact, some lay leaders expressed resentment that a number of today's professionals seem to overshadow their volunteer leaders. As one put it, "ask people in the know, and they'll name the leader of ADL, for example, as Abe Foxman, but they will not know ADL's lay chair's name." Others gave similar examples, berating this development, and concluding that the leadership equation "was out of balance insofar as lay leaders go." In their opinion, volunteers had given over too much power to professionals. Many respondents, especially from the UJA sector, believed that the federation executives had taken over the process.

However, a couple of lay respondents mitigated the often harsh criticisms of federation executives. They thought that the increased role of executives came about because of the abdication of responsibility by lay people. In part, the belief that far fewer lay leaders were knowledgeable enough to play consistent and engaged leadership roles compounded this situation. This, as one long-timer put it, "is inevitable when the professional has come to know so much more than lay leaders." In the past, he continued, "professionals and lay leaders both learned together and trusted one another."

In the opinion of a number of lay leaders we interviewed, they could go elsewhere with their talents and dollars (with much less strife) and take on leadership roles in these new settings. "Options for leadership outside of Jewish life have grown enormously," one disgruntled lay leader said. They often gained greater recognition outside the Jewish community, accompanied by a smaller dollar price tag for their leadership. Yet a number observed that, if one remained involved in Jewish life, lay leadership had to look to staff for guidance.

"Ambivalence" defined how a number of laypersons described their feelings toward professionals. Yet almost everyone spoke with admiration of those federation executives who were seen as strong, knowledgeable, and actively involved in the merger process. Without their involvement, it was said, the process would have disintegrated. The respect given, however, was offered grudgingly. Many voiced concern that lay power had diminished as a result of the merger process. One lay leader commented that this had happened "as much because lay leaders were not sufficiently knowledgeable rather than having had their power and roles usurped by the professionals."

Simultaneously, some noted how professionals "destroyed each other in this process." The very same professionals who insisted so strongly on having an executive chosen from among their ranks, then turned on whichever of their peers was chosen as the chief executive officer. This comment mirrored the opinion expressed by most national CEOs.

The desire to bring in a lay leader from outside the current system as the primary CEO was accompanied by the intention of some to also bring in an executive from "outside." This proposal was tried and modified in response to the outcries of some of the executives who insisted that one of their own be appointed.

# INCORPORATING THE DIVERSITY OF RESPONSES: PROFESSIONALS AND THEMES

From the study, we identified the five most frequently mentioned reasons for a new organization. The core goals for merger, as reflected in the study, are:

1. bringing cost-saving measures and efficiencies to the operation of the national system;

2. securing control of the national system by the federations;

3. establishing a baseline of support for overseas allocations;

4. creating a new national American Jewish voice; and,

5. addressing the governance issues associated with both the UIA and UJA.

Not everyone accepted these goals, and, indeed, they differ somewhat from the prime factors educed by the consultants earlier in the process (see p. 25).

## PERCEPTIONS ON PROCESS

The literature on mergers addresses questions of "shared outcomes" as an essential ingredient in shaping these types of negotiations. From the comments selected here and noted elsewhere, one can identify elements of frustration and the levels of disconnect among a number of the key parties to these discussions.

**Viewing this Process as a Federation Power Play:**

Many respondents from all sectors identified the merger as a "federation-owned" system. Most viewed the drive for merger as a fight for control over the system between federation leaders and UJA representatives. Implied in these observations were, as one UIA activist concluded, "several...forces that brought about the merger. . . .The federation leadership believed they could effect cost reduction in the overall (UJA) national system and gain some control of the overseas allocations/distributions." In turn, the UJA leadership (including Jewish Agency representatives) believed they could access the federation system and stem the erosion and diversion of overseas allocations. What is suggested by these varied expectations is that the federations and the existing national system could not develop shared goals or a shared vision for the new entity.

**Failure to Create an Inclusive National Jewish Entity:**

Almost every one concurred that when the merger was effectuated, it resulted in the UJC becoming the exclusive instrument of the federations, thereby missing an opportunity to become a more representative and inclusive national body. An individual, who initially opposed the merger and later came to favor it, expressed his desire "for an American Jewish voice to counter the Conference of Presidents." This person had envisioned an entity that would allow for the involvement of the religious movements and Zionist institutions on a new board of directors, providing a "truly representative body of American Jewry."

Mergers often fail to achieve the visionary elements that are seen by some as the essential purpose for launching institutional change. This was a case example in which those who sought to create a transformation in communal life believed that the outcomes fell short of their expectations.

**Trust Issues – Failing to Understand the Impact of Local Needs and Services:**

Trust is a central element in the literature on mergers. If players are unable to establish common ground at the outset, many times the merger struggles to achieve broad-based support. Such an inability to establish trust was, on some level, the case here. This judgment was sadly evident when we examined the serious disconnect on the issue of local needs and services

The demand by donors for increased community-based services was mentioned by a significant number of respondents. Demographic shifts resulted in more dramatic demands at the community level to expand services to the elderly, single parents, and pre-school aged children. Similarly, the fall-out over the increased rates of intermarriage, coupled with the response encouraging more expensive day schools, camping experiences and trips to Israel, created additional demands for allocating more dollars to local services for which community leaders turned to their local federations.

As noted earlier, many community-oriented respondents were startled and then angered at the apparent insensitivity of the UJA and UIA leadership to these growing domestic considerations. Conversely, the latter viewed the claims regarding local needs as another ploy to siphon off dollars that rightly ought to be going to meet overseas needs. All this was taking place during a period of stagnant campaigns. In general, the only time campaigns surged was during periods of international crisis. Emergency and special campaigns for Israel as well as Soviet, Ethiopian, and most recently, Argentinean Jewry not only supported these efforts but also freed up dollars to meet local needs. Rather than seeing this as a win-win outcome, some UJA supporters were convinced that federations were, as one person defined it, "stealing" dollars intended for overseas priorities to be used for underwriting local services. Not only does such a comment reflect distrust, it also betrays a deep misunderstanding of the serious issues addressed locally by the federations.

The "trust issue" generated other strains as well as negative consequences. For many participants, the outcome resulted in a significant loss of trust between all the "players" in the merger process. "The present merger arrangement has resulted in creating a structure with uneven functions and competing organizational cultures," noted one respondent. Another participant saw the level of carping among key players as leading to further destabilization or at least the slowing of a successful transition process. The effects, he believed, could be seen in the level of leadership turnover and the exiting of senior staff from the system.

# EXAMINING CULTURAL AND INSTITUTIONAL DISCONNECTS

We uncovered numerous instances of reactions to the differences in organizational culture. UJA participants were critical, sometimes disdainful, of what one of them called the "ponderous pachyderm," i.e., the process-laden character of the federation system. In their opinion, layers of committees in that system compromised the pace of decision-making, all in the name of "process." At the same time, some cynically suggested that this represented a way to insure the indispensability of staff in order for the communal system to operate.

Federations have developed a series of checks and balances through their allocations committees. In contrast, UJA allocations, according to the federation and UIA respondents, were not subjected to the same deliberative process. Traditionally, a small group within each community, operating behind closed doors, negotiated the percentage for overseas distribution. Increasingly, many federation leaders expressed concern that not only was there little accountability in creating the UJA budget but it was also not subject to appropriate oversight.

Simultaneously, on the national level, dissimilar organizational cultures and decision-making styles had evolved. CJF reflected local federation structures by being seen as process-driven and democratic. Over the course of time, in response to its mandate, the CJF created committees to meet the various functional needs of the federated system, in contrast to the more centralized UJA management approach. One respondent concluded that while the CJF "processed things to death," UJA's focus and mission was clear: to identify needs overseas with a particular focus on Israel while nurturing the major donors within the communities. Decisions within the UJA tended to be made swiftly by a few people and implemented without the type of accountability and evaluation process found within the federation system. UJA was not accountable in a similar manner to any core constituency. In the opinion of many local leaders, it lacked a transparent budget.

Unless the key partners to merger deal with these "cultural realities" at the initial stages, it is difficult, according to management experts, to construct a level playing field at the end of the process that is both comfortable and accessible for all parties.

**Realizing the Forces of Time and History:**

Some of our respondents suggested that the impact of the Holocaust and the founding of the State of Israel were seen by some Jews as distant memories. Leaders who had previously been involved and their progeny were moving away from Jewish life in general and more specifically from federation and UJA, viewing these institutions as less relevant.

**Changing Character of Jewish Leadership:**

A number of UJA respondents commented on the present level and quality of leadership, saying that today too few people, including both professionals and lay leaders, realize that, as one put it, "Jewish leaders… [can] move from organization to organization and think beyond the walls of any of their respective organizations. It is a 'shandeh' that we have been unsuccessful in sustaining the involvement of key leaders."

**Successful Moments, Unsuccessful Outcomes:**

There were highlights associated with the merger process. In the opinion of one executive, the Chicago meeting outside of O'Hare Airport represented one such experience because of the "brilliant facilitation" of Dr. Howard Rieger (who assumed the presidency of UJC in the fall of 2004). In general, however, this executive viewed constant complaining as the norm. The result was destructive to the ultimate outcome and injurious to the process.

**Some Snapshot Findings:**

A number of respondents were complimentary of the stages of negotiations, describing them as "solid," but subsequently concluded that the execution and implementation of the final product had left "a lot to be desired." Several individuals wanted to allow more time before passing final judgment on the merger process in order for the governance of UJC to be fully developed. One individual, noting the degree of complexity related to constructing a new institutional framework, commented, "Changing a national system is not the same as orchestrating local community change."

For some, however, the outcomes appeared to be clear and final. Several perspectives were offered with reference to evaluating the success of this enterprise. For certain respondents, this represented a "UJA buy-out." Others posed a self-reflecting question, "Why should we have expected a great organization from two dysfunctional ones?"

Certain participants concluded that the wrong model was adopted, and that instead, an effective "trade association" ought to have been created. "Such an organization would have been cheaper and, in turn, allowed communities to participate, as they so desired." Some respondents however suggested that a trade association had in fact been achieved, which was for them a disappointing outcome, as they were anticipating a more embracing, dynamic, and creative national organization.

In attempting to evaluate how leadership perceived the process, one of our questions asked, *"Did you feel the process that produced the merged organization to be a representative one?"* The feedback offered here may provide some additional and interesting reflections on both the process and its outcomes. "This merger must be seen as a contest between elitism and the populist tradition," suggested one participant, and "the outcome remains unclear as to what type of institution has emerged."

Another participant offered the following observation: "The small and intermediate federations were led to believe that the model would be representative and more transparent than it is." Those involved in intermediate and small cities were most vocal in their opposition to the crafting of this current structure. Their criticism became more pronounced when some of the small and intermediate federation participants were not invited to serve on the newly constituted UJC board with ongoing membership, as had been the practice at the CJF.

Regardless of affiliation, all participants shared the desire for a greater involvement of young people. No one saw where the merger had produced its intended result in this area.

The question, *"Did people from any particular organization seem to dominate the merger efforts?"* was designed to help us understand the cultural and personality factors in the merger discussions. We sought to examine the applicability of the literature regarding possible patterns of domination in the merger process itself. The responses here, as elsewhere, reflected the particular organizational "perspectives" of the respondent, so that UJA-types were identified as not "process-oriented," "controlling," and "outlasting" their "opponents," while CJF lay leaders and large city federation executives were described by certain UJA-affiliated leaders as "dominating" and correspondingly "too focused on process."

When we asked: *"Who were the most active players in the merger process?"* our respondents all pointed to their other organizational counterparts as being the dominant element. The literature suggests that despite certain key commonalties or beliefs associated with the goals for merger, differences in approach and culture drive the various phases of the negotiation process and how specific players respond (Golinsky and DeRuiter, 2002). This pattern was most evident in this case study. For such enterprises to be successful, an agreement around mission and shared values must first be present in order to achieve consensus among key stakeholders. This was not the case here and marks another reason why there appears to be so much dissatisfaction with the UJC.

The question, *"What general lessons did you learn from the merger process?"* produced a variety of responses that confirmed some of the findings offered by LaPiana (1997; 2000) and others. Some of our respondents admitted that they "did not understand the reason for merger or the mission for this new entity." Others evaluated the process itself as "fair, highly participatory, and well run." By contrast, a leader suggested that one needed to pose the question "Are we in better shape today than when we first began this process?" Almost in response, another offered the following commentary: "The unity of the Jewish people must wait for the Messiah."

The respondents interviewed for this study almost unanimously acknowledged that the resulting "product," did not meet their expectations. More strikingly to us was the discovery that the architects of the UJC were never certain about what they had actually intended to create. While there were numerous concepts about the future mission of this national entity, in the end, there was an absence of a shared vision among the key actors in the process. This first step was essential in order to bring about an institutional model reflecting the type and quality of change desired by the primary stakeholders.

The outcomes envisioned by the various constituencies were never achieved. Why? Several factors came into play. The stakeholders themselves represented competing interests. This failure to shape and/or share a common vision was never adequately addressed by the core participants. The discussions on merger covered several sequences, representing a series of different initiatives, which

63

occurred over time. As these discussions moved forward, a series of players would participate at various stages, resulting in what is described as a non-linear process.

A central element necessary for constructing a resilient, sustainable merger must involve establishing common base points upon which to build trust and to frame an agreed upon plan of action. The initial period of distrust and disruption, as referenced in the literature, must ultimately be replaced by a climate of comfort and trust.

How the different participants interact with one another throughout the stages of negotiation must be seen as critical to the overall success of mergers. The compatibility or relationship factor represents a second core ingredient. The engagement of the core participants in all phases of the merger process represents in the end a critical component to the successful outcome of such discussions.

# CREATING CLASSIFICATIONS

In addition to organizational affiliation and professional status, we grouped interviewees, both lay and professional according to the nature of their responses. In our third classification of the interview material, we identified various themes among the different respondents and organized them with basic labels. The classifications devised for the purposes of this study include: **"localists," "fiscal watchdogs," "internationalists,"** and **"visionaries."** Below we describe each of these groupings:

## Localists

This group of respondents included those primarily active on the local level. Many of these individuals had been involved with local agencies or synagogues as well as their federation boards, while also serving on the CJF board. All had been to Israel and were committed to maintaining allocations to the Jewish State. Their concerns were related to the equitable distribution of allocable dollars as well as more accountability in the decision-making process.

Since the Six Day War in 1967, allocations to Israel had increased dramatically. Over the years "localists" saw the allocation formula of roughly 70/30 (70% for overseas and 30% to local needs) as unfair. Over the last decades, these allocation ratios have been radically shifted in the direction of support for community-based needs and services.

This cohort concentrated on the array of issues dominating the communal agenda: poverty and unemployment; single parents and their unique needs; assimilation and intermarriage; the increased costs of Jewish living and its affect on middle and lower class families; decreased affiliation rates; and an aging population requiring a myriad of increasingly expensive and comprehensive services. Many saw JDC and JAFI as already responding to many similar concerns in Israel and countries throughout the world. They were sympathetic to these international realities but believed that their primary responsibility should be focused on their local constituencies.

At the same time, localists frequently pointed out that the dollars raised in the name of the UJA were raised within the communities. They wanted to "own" the system in order to insure a balanced or "fair share" use of resources.

There were those within this group who voiced a desire to "own the system" for other reasons. As we indicated previously, these respondents believed a double standard existed. Local services were subjected to intensive review through the communities' budgeting and allocations process, while many of these individuals believed such was not the case on the national and international level. In the opinion of these respondents, a political process controlled the distribution of overseas dollars. In the opinion of these localists, the agreed-upon formula did not reflect core needs but rather the amounts, which could be negotiated within each federation, and in turn, with the UJA. In the end, this group supported a strong and viable Israel but not at the expense of being unresponsive to local needs and services.

**Fiscal Watchdogs**

These respondents were drawn from many of the same organizations as the localists. The title "fiscal watchdogs" reflected this group's primary concern for efficiency along with the specific intent to "streamline" the national system. In their minds, the system was constrained by overlapping and needlessly competing functions. They viewed the national organizations with some degree of suspicion, believing that key national professionals were overpaid. They wanted dollars to be saved, though they often could not articulate a clear context for realizing these savings. Merger was seen as a positive outcome if it could demonstrate cost-savings. As one respondent noted, "It was time to clean up the barn." About a fifth of the respondents shared this as their primary concern.

Rarely did the "fiscal watchdogs" raise the issue of effectiveness as a separate outcome for the merger but rather introduced these concerns around overlapping functions and accountability as part of the broader agenda. They tended to share the philosophy and concerns of the localists. The great majority of the localists and the fiscal watchdogs identified with the CJF as a service system for local federations.

**Internationalists**

Most of these respondents had initially been active in their local federations, Zionist organizations and/or synagogues. They became involved on the national and international levels, most frequently through the UIA and UJA. Many had achieved leadership-level positions within these organizations.

These were the strong advocates for overseas dollars, mostly on behalf of JAFI rather than JDC. They pointed out that the growth of federation campaigns over the past decades was a direct result of overseas crises, especially in Israel. They specifically believed that local federations were "raising dollars on the backs of Israel." The great crises of the Jewish people during this period, including the evacuation of thousands of Ethiopians Jews and the absorption of one million Soviet Jews in Israel, had resulted in a number of successful emergency campaigns. These respondents believed that local federations had made these issues central to their fund raising but not central to the allocation's process outside of these emergency appeals.

They frequently voiced impatience with the "process approach" of local federations as described elsewhere. In the end, they believed that the ability of these national entities to act quickly, without interminable committees and layers of meetings, was unique and played a special role in Jewish life. They also believed that the issues and causes with which these agencies identified brought passion to Jewish communal life. In many instances, the UIA participants in this study tended to confirm the UJA leadership's assessment of local federations and their leaders.

For the internationalists, Israel represents a special place in the collective heart of the Jewish people. Without a secure and stable Israel, all would be lost for Jewish life everywhere. Israel and its concerns had to be central to the efforts of local federations. Among those we labeled "internationalists," the overseas respondents tended to be the most ideological and passionate. As indicated previously, few from this sector favored the merger.

Individuals loyal to the UJA feared that the downward slide of dollars allocated to Israel could not be stopped. There were, however, other internationalist voices; individuals involved with the CJF who shared the same set of concerns as their UJA counterparts. While this cohort did not represent significant numbers in our overall study, their views deviated from the preponderant position held by those we labeled "localists." This group recognized the increased demand on federation dollars at the local level, yet had concluded that there needed to be a guaranteed threshold of overseas allocations, at least for a fixed period of years. As a result, they joined the internationalists in advocating such a plan, after which point the allocation's process and percentages would be reviewed.

## Visionaries

In addition to these three groups, there were less than a handful of people drawn from both the professional and volunteer ranks who envisioned this moment in American Jewish history as a rare opportunity to make radical changes in the conduct of "Jewish business." We have labeled this cohort the "visionaries."

On the whole, the various responses to the concept of merger, regardless of organizational affiliation, can best be described as essentially defensive. Regardless of primary identification, there were few who saw the merger as an opportunity to design a truly new kind of national organization. Of all the respondents, we identified five, regardless of organizational affiliation and lay or professional background, who we have called "visionaries." They saw the creation of a new national body as presenting unique possibilities for addressing the broader needs of the Jewish people.

Having observed over two decades the failed attempts at creating merger, one leader described these prior initiatives as motivated by the desire on the part of federation (both lay and professional), to control, not only the dollars but also the relations with Israel. These motivations, he felt, were over and above any drive for more efficiency. In previous decades, this individual had resisted other attempts at merger. Yet, he had come to see the possibilities of a new synergy as a result of the creation of the UJC. He saw at this time new challenges to Jewish life, including the need both for more Jewish communal professionals and also for a more unified approach to raising significantly larger sums of money for overseas, national, and local needs. He felt this would be possible with a centralized philanthropic fundraising model and a unified national system of decision-making. He was hesitant at first – "fearful," as he put it – that "UJA would lose its independence, but I came to feel its functions could benefit [from the merger] in the long run."

He saw the changing attitudes toward Israel among young people in his own community and believed the merger would help to pull them closer to the Jewish state. Correspondingly, this individual believed the new structure of the UJC had been misunderstood. He saw this initiative as an opportunity to bring current leadership closer to the national and overseas scene.

Another respondent suggested that the new entity would bring "relevant" leadership into governance roles, while the new structure of pillars (the designated fields of interest through which UJC's business was to be conducted) would provide opportunities for young leaders to be closer to issues central to the Jewish people, including Israel, education, human services, etc.

This same person thought the new structure had the opportunity to involve more people, as was initially intended. But the implementation was aborted by a subsequent dismantling of the system, immediately after the merger. "Presently, no budget process or substance in the new organization exists to retain people's interest." His thoughts reflected the beliefs and suggestions made by this small cohort of visionaries.

Other individuals within this category regretted not having religious and Zionist representatives included in the newly-constituted board. They thought that the UJC could have developed new funding sources for recruiting, training, and placing professionals in the field. Most argued that a significant increase in the number and dollar value of national scholarships was needed. The majority wanted as well a mega-scholarship fund for day schools, camps, and Israel experiences. They believed that opportunities were missed to develop new venues for involving people in governance. The creation of a national training center for lay people and professionals was proposed by two of these respondents. A research and development fund was necessary in their opinion to foster change and growth within Jewish life. Many from this group regretted the loss of the UJA name. In general, this group posited a wide range of creative and challenging ideas designed to reset the national agenda.

# INSTITUTIONAL LOSS – THE FIVE C'S

Any merger involves change and loss. The blending of capacities, skills, and resources invariably reveals expected (and unexpected) benefits as well as unintended blemishes. The creation of the UJC uncovered a series of problems that affected the respondents' judgment of the merger. Many interviewees, for example, criticized the loss of senior lay and professional leaders, the former being dropped or disfranchised as a result of the merger. With regard to the latter, numerous senior professionals left the national system.

Moreover, many local federation leaders identified as an unmet expectation the failure of the merger to eliminate waste and reduce expenditures. One respondent commented, "In the end we failed to achieve either cost savings or economies of scale. . . ." (It should be noted that since these comments were offered, the UJC has taken significant steps to reduce its budget and improve its fiscal practices.)

A significant number of community representatives argued that federations, especially the intermediate and small city communities, suffered a loss of services as a consequence of the merger. Qualitative services formerly provided by the CJF and UJA (consultative services, including planning and public relations functions, professional development, and financial resource development programs) were not in place post-merger to assist communities. Furthermore, the new board structure deprived the smaller federations of an automatic seat at the table. In addition, federation system partners, such as the Jewish Educational Services of North America (JESNA) and the Jewish Council for Public Affairs (JCPA), were viewed as having lost some of their institutional autonomy to operate outside of the new national system as a result of the merger.

These problems and the judgments they produced among the interviewees were symptomatic of a series of core concerns that the participants had expressed. They are:

## Consensus

The Jewish communal system was built on the consensus model, where policy and process were governed by the principles of shared engagement. Leadership collectively framed the goals and directions of this enterprise. In our discussions with a number of national and local leaders, there was a serious concern over the loss of the consensus model in decision-making. "We failed to rebuild the consensus process and, in the process, we lost critical sets of relationships with key leaders," one respondent noted. A number of our respondents commented on the emergence of a corporate model in the Jewish communal system in recent years which has resulted in an erosion of institutional participation and a disengagement of specific leadership elements.

## Credibility

"Credibility has been lost, and it needs to be regained." Respondents suggested several areas where there are specific credibility concerns. On the one hand, certain community federations and partner national agencies, in particular JDC, are alienated. On the other hand, there are former influential national leaders who feel disconnected and disempowered as a result of the new UJC governance system.

## Connections

"Key stakeholders are not present with dollars, time or energy." While tied to the earlier reference regarding credibility, here respondents were also suggesting that the UJC needed to attract those donors who have moved away from centralized giving. Another expression of concern about the attenuation of connections is found in the following assessment: "Due to the structural issues inherent within the UJC , no new leadership could emerge."

## Communications

The techniques for constructing a new system of governance required more effective communications. As one stakeholder stated, "we were in too big of a hurry to realize that we missed some vital pieces to the process." Mattessich and Monsey (1992), in their work on institution building, have suggested that the communications apparatus is particularly important in collaborative/merger processes, citing the need to create "open and frequent communication" through both informal and formal links. Many individuals commented in their interviews that they believed that, at the outset of the creation of the new entity, the communications' networks of the organization were not adequately structured. This resulted in "information shortfall" and "power outages" among the key national participants and the communities.

## Culture

The cultural framework of an organization is found in the manner in which it pursues its goals and values its mission. According to one source, culture-building within the merger process centered on "cost savings. . . .[We] failed to look at the 'big picture.'" Another community leader described the cultural environment as lacking passion, "the kishkas of the lay people was not there." Others described the institutional imperative here as conceived by some leaders as seeking a new constellation based on the principle that "bigger is better," that the size of the new agency was more important than the results it achieved.

# THE PERCEIVED LOSERS

## Status of Women

Remarkably few people commented about the changing role of women in Jewish life. Many of those interviewed for this study are active in trying to break the "glass ceiling" for women. Among our respondents, the fact that this issue did not arise could have been due to the focus on the merger and its processes. The continued relative infrequency of women in senior executive roles was never referred to. A growing (though still small) number of women have risen to high posts within the voluntary sector and were involved in the merger process. None of them commented on the absence of women among the professionals, however. We hope this issue is addressed in an accelerated and more serious manner, and we offer this observation in that spirit.

## UJC

From the beginning of the merger talks, some respondents believed that the "UJC was doomed to disappoint almost every one from the outset. A highly placed executive commented that not only were the roles of professional and lay leaders blurred but that the leadership had not established a shared vision. The UJC was "preordained to fail," according to this source. This respondent believed that the merger "produced anarchy in the name of unity." American Friends of JAFI (the new North American Council) and JDC have been empowered to go their own way in America as a result of the merger. He opined that all national organizations that had been formerly coordinated under the CJF umbrella had been "let loose" to go on their own, resulting in the loss of a coordinated national structure to effectively serve the Jewish community.

In the opinion of one national executive, "UJC has experienced a melt down. It will be back to square one, not having accomplished its intended purpose to be a powerful force on the American scene.

It has lost its power and its purpose." It was the viewpoint of some participants and observers that not all leaders involved in the merger or post-merger process really understood the complexities of the national system.

## UIA

Those individuals identified as UIA leaders felt betrayed by the results of the merger. They reluctantly agreed to the merger out of a sense of resignation, coupled with a desire to ensure a continuing level of financial support for overseas concerns. They were given initial assurances that they would be expected to cooperate in effectuating savings through shared facilities, administrative services and the like, while maintaining their institutional independence. In their opinion, the functions of the UIA were unique, non-duplicative, and essential to the infrastructure of Jewish communal life. In the end, UIA leaders believed that they were not truly involved in merger discussions or treated as a partner; they were simply acquired. Their unique role and governance structure was now lost.

## Israel

In the opinion of one respondent, Israel represents one of the principal losers, as the UJC was not in a position to sustain its level of overseas financial engagement. In the view of some, the UJC will not be a strong enough national instrument with sufficient power to balance local needs and international priorities. A related question involved those local federations which have expanded their own operations in Israel, bypassing the UJC altogether. Meanwhile, the increased frequency of directed giving by large donors might ultimately weaken the capacity of this new system to achieve its core objectives. This trend in individualized giving has allowed JDC and JAFI, among other international funding entities, to develop relatively autonomous power in America when the intended outcome was designed for more accountability from all parties.

## UJA

There was no consistent criticism of the process itself offered by UJA participants, most had reluctantly agreed to the merger process, thinking this was their last chance to strengthen support for overseas needs.

### Downgrading of the UJA Overseas Mission

A number of people most identified with the UJA saw its role severely diminished as a result of the merger. A number of respondents concurred with UIA participants that, by curtailing core functions associated with the UIA, the UJC had eliminated a possible venue within the federated system where other institutional voices of American Jewry, namely, the religious and Zionist organizations, might have played a role. Many UJA respondents believed that subsequent to the merger, ONAD did not provide a consistent voice on behalf of the needs of Israel and the international agenda to the same degree as UJA exhibited when it was a separate entity.

### Other Institutional Losers

Several executives observed that small and intermediate federations experienced a loss of institutional influence as a result of the configuration of power within the UJC system. As mentioned earlier, their rotational roles on the new board, as compared to the permanent place and power of the large federations, diminished their access and denied their lay leadership significant and sustained participation.

JDC and JAFI: The focus of most local federations regarding the distribution and use of overseas dollars was much more centered on JAFI than with the JDC. Yet, the latter's mission was understood with greater clarity by the communities as it was seen as an American-based organization. Similarly, as there were fewer dollars involved, federations generally responded more favorably to JDC, its mission, board, and staff.

## The Consultants

The consulting firms did not actually understand the issues and possibilities that might have been pursued. Many believe these outside companies were forced upon the participants by a small group of well-intentioned Jewish donors. Instead of focusing on the underlying issues of change (e.g., mission, vision, values, culture, etc.), the consultants directed the process on how to develop an "acceptable" new organization.

Underscoring the general unhappiness with the outcome, a large number of respondents who were a part of one or more of the participating institutions thought they were losers in the merger process. Indeed, another substantial group suggested that there were no winners at all! However, a number of participants identified specific winners (as well as losers).

The literature on various corporate and nonprofit mergers suggests that there is a tendency on the part of those who were shut out of the benefits of a merger to view the process as having failed. Others with specific interests, who perceive that their concerns were not readily or adequately addressed in the new format, will often describe the outcome as flawed. This was certainly the case in our findings.

For many respondents, the notion of "winners" seemed difficult, if not impossible, to define. A level of cynicism colored the perspective of some who suggested that former UJA and CJF personnel who received substantial severance packages or buy-outs actually might have been the true winners. A few of those surveyed concluded that the UJA/Overseas programs, as reflected in the emergency campaign initiatives for Israel and Argentina, along with Partnership 2000, could be identified as victors. In supporting this notion, one observer commented, "UJA was resurrected from the dead." This conclusion was contrary to the view of most UJA leadership.

In answering the question: "Did any one of the organizations involved in the merger benefit more than the other?" we received responses that reflected the institutional allegiances of the respective participants. As might have been anticipated, many representing the CJF and federation constituencies concluded that the UJA, its culture, content, and collaborators all benefited, while

UJA representatives believed that the outcome produced a CJF victory. A number of respondents noted that UJC's mission was the last item to be addressed within the merger process. As a result, the outcome may still be in doubt as to which party or agenda might benefit. Many noted the lack of passion within the UJC upon the loss of UJA's name, mission, and national prominence.

**Federations**

The large city federations were frequently identified as the potential winners. The UJC was seen as specifically designed to serve their interests. "The power has shifted to the large federations and to their executives who today make the critical decisions," one national Jewish leader put it. Another prominent activist offered the following assessment: "Fearful of losing their power and concerned about protecting the status quo, the large city federation executives took power."

Most understood that the local federations ended up "owning the system." A significant number of UJA leaders believed that "UIA's time had passed" and did not lament its absorption into the process. Many former UJA leaders were convinced that they were shut out of the new structure and that the development was orchestrated by the CJF (read federation) leadership. The merger was made possible because of the sanction and pressure of local professional and lay leaders, resulting in the tilting of the traditional balance of power involving lay and professional leadership to the federation executives. This, in the opinion of a senior professional, resulted in large city federation executives securing "ownership" over the new system.

**JDC**

JDC was viewed by almost everyone as an effective and efficient organization. It was perceived that the Joint does what it wants to do with no real oversight or accountability to a central body. It was the view of some that it would not be too late however "to rein in" JDC.

Even as they complimented JDC, several respondents found that "it was a little too independent at times." Preliminary discussions among the leaders of CJF, UIA and UJA resulted in the decision not to include JDC as part of a newly-merged organization. Apparently, according to this observer, JDC's leadership engaged in a serious discussion about the advantages and disadvantages of becoming part of the merger discussions, concluding it would not be to its advantage to participate. A number of people concluded that JDC, in the end, benefited more than any other organization. One respondent believed that, if anything, JDC had been able to take advantage of the new allocation process. It also may conduct more open fundraising in America than it was previously allowed to undertake. While the combined budgets of the three merged organizations have been cut by nearly $6 million, the JDC has grown by virtue of having a freer hand in raising dollars in its own name even as it continues to receive an allocation through ONAD.

## OVERVIEW COMMENTS

Any analysis of the UJC merger will sadly conclude that many of the principles that undergird successful mergers were missing or insufficiently followed during the process. According to Thomas McLaughlin (1998), the essentials necessary for success in structuring merger are:

- mutual exploration and analysis;
- synthesis and tentative planning;
- a working committee structure;
- quick victories;
- institutional buy-in;
- a work plan for each area of the alliance; and,
- a formalized operational structure.

One would need to question the level of mutual exploration and analysis undertaken by the discussants at the beginning of the merger negotiating process. A more focused examination of the core issues, possibilities, and problems might have ultimately generated a shared vision, greater collective buy-in, and a diminished set of negative challenges to the system in the end.

In hindsight, one might suggest that the absence of "quick victories" (principle four) represented a key missing symbolic element that might have been particularly important in containing the UJC's critics and turning around potential institutional problems. Similarly, the absence of "institutional buy-in" may represent the central institutional crisis facing UJC. Echoing McLaughlin, one respondent suggested the following reflective comment: "To change cultures takes more time and maybe we rushed too quickly into the implementation phase." A number of those who assessed the merger product believed that the absence of an operational structure (principle seven) represented, as one critic would suggest, "the defining missing component" of the merger discussions.

# JEWISH VALUES, SOCIAL TRENDS, AND BUSINESS PRACTICES

## Jewish Values as Points of Reference

Jewish communal organizations must be seen as sacred spaces and the tasks undertaken by its leadership as holy work. Accordingly, Jewish organizational leaders must see their roles not only as trustees of the institutional mantle but also to insure that new outcomes serve communal interests. The insights and values offered by Jewish tradition can serve as benchmarks for the UJC and the larger communal system. Identified below are a few core themes extracted from Jewish texts that might serve as guideposts.

- **Honesty:** We are commanded by our tradition to seek the truth and to correct that which is evil (Exodus 20:18) and we are taught that we must speak out against all forms of defamation. "They that deal truly are God's delight." (Proverbs 12:22)

- **Integrity:** "Mark the person of integrity, and behold the upright." (Psalms 37:37)

- **Loyalty:** "Honor thy father and thy mother that thy days may be long upon the land which the Lord thy God giveth thee. (Exodus 20:12)

- **Tzedakah:** (Justice): "Seek justice and relieve the oppressed." (Isaiah 1:17)

- **Chesed:** (Compassion): "Show mercy and compassion, everyone to your neighbor." (Zechariah: 7:9)

- **Respect for Human Dignity:** Human beings were created in the image of God, thus each individual is deserving of respect as a unique creature of God.

- **Respect for Law:** "The law of the state is the law." (Gittin 10b)

- **Accountability for Actions and Decisions:** According to the tradition, we are responsible for accepting responsibility for all our decisions and actions, whether carried out intentionally or inadvertently, and for setting an example for other people. (Mishnah Baba Kamma, 1:12)

## Social Trends and Business Practices as Benchmarks

In defining the Jewish future, one must also assess a set of "mega" trends that represent the significant ideas that will dominate the social landscape over the coming years. Several generic themes should be seen as significant to this report:

- **Privatization, individualism, and competition** represent defining elements of American society and the nonprofit sector.

- **Multiple centers of power and energy** reflect American diversity as well as the realities associated with Jewish life in the 21$^{st}$ century.

- **Experimentation with collaboration** speaks to the countervailing element in American society that, despite the themes of individualism and the presence of competing organizational voices, the most creative and risk-prepared institutions are those willing to test new ways of organizing and managing resources in partnership with others from both the business and nonprofit arenas.

Further, we think that the six business-related practices listed below reflect the changing character of the nonprofit sector and more directly that of the Jewish communal system. As the UJC seeks to define and clarify its role, these concepts may help inform and direct its institutional practices:

- **Economies of Scale:** Replacing the randomness of choices that traditionally dominated community practice with more targeted and engaged financial resource initiatives and management-based systems of governance and decision making.

- **Management Systems:** strategic thinking and business planning will drive organizational practice.

84

- **Research and Development:** Any serious institutional decision making will be guided by the R/D functions of an organization.

- **Risk-Taking:** Even in an age of increased institutional accountability, there will be a premium placed on testing and experimentation.

- **Marketing Strategies:** As the Jewish community becomes more geographically dispersed and demographically segmented, organizations will need to aggressively pursue the tools of creative marketing.

- **Leadership Orientation:** Leading complex institutions will require a more formalized approach to the training and preparation of both professional executives and board participants in the tasks related to decision-making, planning, and managing.

## Other Reflections on UJC as a Case Study

After surveying key stakeholders, Solomon and Wachsstock (2003) concluded, "UJC is plagued by a lack of clarity of mission, which will seriously hamper its effectiveness." Below is additional material from their study, which adds an important dimension to our research.

- **Structural Change in Society/Economy:** The Jewish communal enterprise has yet to respond effectively to the external structural and economic changes evident in American society.

- **The Shift in Needs:** Past challenges have given way to a focus on hopes and dreams.

- **Change in Donors:** The focus on accountability and applicability of the donor's contribution has altered and diminished the traditional role of the *kehilla* or communal model

- **Transitions in Lay Leadership:** A generation focused on the culture of process has replaced a cadre of wealthy, knowledgeable leaders committed to engaging and working with professionals.

- **Professional Challenge:** Professionals seeking to accommodate to the changes in community leadership can only provide limited leadership, absent bold initiatives and rapid responses.

- **Reshtetlization:** Outside of international crisis, the focus in Jewish life has shifted to local concerns, in some measure countering the push toward national unification.

- **Diversity:** The disconnect between leaders and followers. The composition of both our communal leadership and body politic is undergoing profound change. Influenced and shaped by a new generation of Jewish activists, the presence of "new Jews," those who come to us from other societies and cultures and those who "by choice" are now part of the Jewish people, require our communal systems to adapt to the growing diversity that will define our constituencies.

- **Inclusiveness:** The communal system being seen as exclusive. In many ways, this system is identified as elitist. In the 21$^{st}$ century, it must also demonstrate the characteristics of being a "popularist" structure in its organizational strategies.

- **Quality/Universality:** Competition and sophisticated consumerism, which have reshaped the marketplace, must seriously impact the Jewish communal system.

- **Welcoming Community:** Patterns of consumerism as practiced by Jews is neither understood nor embraced by the Jewish communal network.

## REFLECTIONS ON CHAOS

We have learned much through the course of our study. We find it appropriate to address obvious questions that may have risen about the title of this work. Solomon and Wachsstock's findings are highly congruent with our own research, which further emphasizes the urgent need to apply the recommendations from both studies.

When we began our study, some observers and participants used the word "chaos." Our title represents in one phrase the desire on our part to ascertain what people who were most involved thought about the merger and the process which led to the formation of UJC.

We do not believe there was chaos, but there was confusion and profound differences. Clearly, almost no one was satisfied with the outcome, the creation of the UJC. Many were bitter, some disillusioned. Others had second thoughts, feeling they should have left the existing institutional system in place. A few had great regrets for not pushing harder to create a truly new organization to serve the Jewish people here and abroad. The overarching sentiments were those of disappointment and frustration.

As Jews, we believe that the world is repairable, and as social scientists we know that bright new ideas can emerge from the dark intimations of chaos The same spirit animates our consideration of the UJC. It must be understood as a work in progress, and our findings should help continue the process. . Therefore, we see it as a challenge and a responsibility for the Jewish people to engage fully in this process.

# RECOMMENDATIONS

It is easy to be Monday morning quarterbacks. Those on the playing field face realities to which observers are not privy. At the same time, spectators on the sidelines or up in the press box, can anticipate or see things the players may miss. It is in that spirit that we set forth these observations and recommendations.

These proposals are drawn from the general observations offered to us by those we interviewed. Many of the ideas are extracted from those described earlier as "visionaries." Finally, these observations and recommendations reflect our own views with regard to Jewish life and the future of the communal system.

The proposals are designed to reflect the core elements found in contemporary management literature on mergers and collaborative relationships. The review of the literature demonstrates the inconsistencies, difficulties, and almost inevitable disappointments associated with merger outcomes. We believe that our recommendations can help surmount that outcome.

An equally important framework for understanding the recommendations is rooted in a model of governance that has guided Jews for over two millennia. In one form or another, this model is still found today in most Jewish communal bodies throughout the world, including Israel. At bottom, it functions in an open, disputatious, contentious climate, yet one that respects checks and balances – between wisdom, knowledge, and economic power and/or between judicial, executive, and legislative functions. The literature on the historical values of the *Ketarim* system and the *Kehilla* model will provide useful background to these principles (see Appendices IV and V).

The Recommendations are divided into two primary categories – "Governance and Structure" and "Leadership and Training."

## GOVERNANCE AND STRUCTURE

As an outcome of the merger process, we believe that the UJC has taken a step backward by diminishing the checks and balances traditionally in place in Jewish life. The value of "representativeness" constituted one of the hallmarks of Jewish life in most communities. The elimination of a place at the governance table for key institutional voices has markedly narrowed that traditional model. As a number of respondents pointed out, the result is an anomaly. On the local level, numerous federations have reached out to their synagogues, cosponsoring and funding synagogue-based services and working with and through local boards of rabbis to respond collectively to local, national, and international matters of widespread Jewish concern. Where they exist, local Zionist groups have been included in the communal system.

Not reflecting these developments on the national scene is to ignore or even deny the changes that are at play locally. Federation supporters, fewer in numbers as they may be compared to past decades, tend to be affiliated with synagogues and/or other Jewish organizations. When federations organize or coordinate citywide events, they can only succeed when there is a high level of cooperation with those institutions and organizations. Without these relationships, federations could not produce the mass community rallies needed on occasion to demonstrate Jewish unity.

The absence of academics, intellectuals, and rabbis from the governance process further demonstrates the departure from normative Jewish governance models. We view this as a serious loss for our communal system.

With the exception of the national community relations venue, the Jewish Council for Public Affairs (JCPA), there is a dearth of public forums within federations themselves. This has further diminished the vitality of the governance process. Many respondents felt minority voices were often muted. The honoring of those voices goes back to the time of our rabbinic sages, who understood that today's small voices frequently come to be tomorrow's conventional wisdom.

Many respondents commented on these departures from Jewish norms and practices. Some even cited Jewish text as a reason for their concern about the lack of diversity within our boardrooms. Jews as American citizens are a part of a proud civic heritage. The very engagement of American Jewry within the public square on behalf of constitutional issues such as free speech, minority rights, and open discourse is ironically suspended within the context of Jewish communal life.

In the case of some putatively "radical" recommendations, we hope they will not be dismissed out of hand. Looking at other organizational models does not suggest that full replication could or should be tried. But it should challenge us to think in new ways. Extrapolating the applicable and testing the new opens up opportunities to learn from others about how to structure services or build organizations.

Such is the case with many of our recommendations. We re-emphasize that a number of them came from those we interviewed while others were logical extensions drawn from the extensive and frank discussions engaged in by so many of those we interviewed..

We both want to remind our readers that we are not living in an ivory tower. Both of us serve on a number of boards and committees within the community and have spent a great number of years consulting, observing, conducting research and otherwise participating in Jewish organizational life here and abroad.

Between us we have been called upon to serve as speakers, teachers, and consultants in over 125 communities throughout the world. The perspective we bring is born of the gift we have been given to observe so many different organizations in so many diverse communities and settings.

This opportunity is given to few. We have been able to have these experiences in various kinds of institutions -- centers, synagogues, federations and their counterparts overseas, homes for the aged, family services, planning bodies, community relations organizations, teaching institutions, and a number of national and international organizations.

In addition to our findings, we have drawn upon these experiences, and in that spirit we offer our recommendations for review and assessment.

**1. Restore the UJA Name for Public and Federation use Country-wide:**

A significant number of respondents from within all groups bemoaned the loss of the UJA "brand" name. Independent marketing experts confirmed this conclusion, feeling strongly that a familiar name was lost. The new name, "United Jewish Communities," does not convey the organization's mission. Ironically, the federation system, perceived as the new "owners," has not gained a new national identity as a consequence of the process.

We do not suggest at this point that we have an appropriate new name. However, a few communities in metropolitan New Jersey and New York have included UJA as part of their organization's name. Surely expert marketers could help in this process. It would seem to be an important consideration. Establishing a national department of UJA reflecting the local model of United Jewish Funds should be easy to implement.

## 2. Examine a New Model for the UJC and Its Relations to Local Federations:

The UJC has been described as a trade association by a number of respondents. It is a creation developed mostly by local federation leadership. This resonates to the structure that has been in place for the last one hundred and ten years. In our opinion, a more appropriate model worthy of serious examination would be a national certification system with local affiliates.

A national organization, also a century old, has moved to the type of model that we are introducing here for consideration. Big Brothers Big Sisters of America (BBBSA), itself a merger of two national organizations, is structured as a certification system. Each community-based agency has its own independent 501(c)3 status and is incorporated locally. Each community organization has its own board of directors, with the authority to set policy, hire and fire personnel, and control its priorities and programs. In turn, the national office of BBBSA controls its own brand name, encourages pilot projects to determine best practices in a variety of service and fundraising areas and funds them. In order to be sanctioned, with full rights and privileges, service standards must be met by each local agency. Only then can the national logo and brand name be utilized.

BBBSA national board members include nationally prominent figures and representatives from the leadership of local agencies. In addition, national evaluative research is conducted and fully funded through this central structure. Centralized lobbying is conducted in Washington, D.C. in order to acquire federal monies, which are then distributed to local agencies on a proportional basis, supplementing community fundraising. Training for both volunteers and professional staff is provided by the national office via on-line materials and regional and national gatherings. Areas covered include fundraising, marketing, service delivery, staff development, and volunteer training.

Finally, the national office manages advertising and marketing strategies. The national system has two primary campaign goals: to attract potential volunteers and to secure contributions for the local BBBSA. The volunteers are automatically referred to their local agency based on their zip code, while contributions are distributed in the same manner. The production of marketing products adaptable to local needs allows for the highest quality of uniformly recognized material, shaped for unique community purposes.

If this model or some similar one were adopted, every local federation in the United States would have the same name, logo, and brand. This represents a radical departure from the present federated system. At the least, UJC leadership might meet with national BBBSA leadership and other certification operations to ascertain the feasibility of working toward such a model.

## 3. Issues of Representation:

• The decision not to place religious movements and other institutional representatives on the board:

The UJC faces a dilemma. For most of the respondents in our study, the UJC has become a "federation-owned" organization. There are those who view it as a "trade association" in new clothing and bemoan that it has become excessively and needlessly narrow. A distinctive pillar was established devoted to educational and programmatic concerns in Jewish life, an area of special interest to many in the Jewish community. While religious movements and Zionist representatives were not considered for board membership at the UJC, they were assigned to this pillar, confirming for many that a significant opportunity had been missed.

The reality is that within communities people don't "belong" to federations, they support them. With rare exceptions, they belong to diverse organizations and institutions. Many belong to synagogues and a significant number to secular Jewish organizations as well. The fact remains, however, that most Jews in America are not formally affiliated with any Jewish organization.

One executive director pointed out the extent to which local federations are increasingly funding aspects of synagogue life and cooperating programmatically with congregations. UJC does not reflect or reinforce these developments. As we have noted elsewhere, the lack of synagogue activists, both lay and rabbinic, within the new structure is a significant omission and represents a missing element central to Jewish civic life.

Differences are present within our community, and they cannot and ought not to be ignored. While not taking particular stands, the UJC must ensure that venues are provided for discussion and debate around the core issues of Jewish life. These missing voices are needed to reflect on these critical questions.

• The expansion of opportunities for wider and more representative involvement of volunteers:

A significant number of interviewees in our study voiced concern about the downward trend in the number of people involved in federations. The UJC itself faces a dilemma: how to streamline an organization by sharply reducing the number of board members and committees while at the same time addressing decreased opportunities for involvement resulting from the merger. Responding to strong pressure nationwide, the immediate past CEO put measures in place which saved millions of dollars annually. Now, leadership faces the challenge to differentiate efficiency from effectiveness. Many of the cost savings were appropriate and should be kept in place. At the same time, appreciating that meaningful involvement of people costs money and requires staff time, leadership should revisit the earlier cuts. The results associated with increased lay participation are often not easily measurable in dollar terms. No one can predict how, when, or if, a lay person will be energized into playing a more significant role (financially and otherwise) as a result of his/her increased involvement in an organization. We all know that it happens. Is it worth the price? We think it is. The UJC is often too removed from its constituencies; expanding opportunities for lay participation may assist in addressing that problem. Finding the balance between investing in people while remaining fiscally prudent is not simple. Yet it is an important goal to pursue.

There is the need to restore the balance called for in the late Daniel Elazar's concept of the three crowns (see Appendix III). The *Baal HaMeah* as *Baal HaDeah* (the wealthy as controllers of the ideas and actions of an organization) has increasingly come to be the norm in Jewish life. We believe that the UJC and the federated system would benefit from the expression of a greater diversity of viewpoints than exists presently.

There are Jewish Nobel Prize winners, university presidents, jurists, and deans with rich and diverse backgrounds who are concerned about the quality and content of Jewish life. Today, the intellectual and artistic community is composed of a disproportionate number of Jews. Jewish writers, academics, and creative artists abound. On occasion, we use them for lectures, read their books, appreciate their art, and take nourishment from their presence in our society. Yet they are largely absent from UJC deliberations. Rarely do we draw on their talents and wisdom in the governance of Jewish life. They are society's critics, observers, and occasion visionaries. They study and reflect who we are, what we do, and how we do it. They are our conscience, lampooning us, moralizing, and critiquing us. We must find ways of bringing them into the tent of organized Jewish life. They often make us uncomfortable, but what would our society and we be without them?

Few from this rich reservoir of talent may want to serve in traditional ways as board and committee members. But the UJC and all federations would do well to find creative ways of making use of their talents in the governing process.

Even as we work to increase voluntarism, it is important to measure our efforts against the maxim that wealth, work, wisdom and "menschlikeit" (acting in a fair and caring manner) are attributes essential for achieving an institutional balance within Jewish communal life. This unique balance remains the norm in most communities abroad and would surely well serve the UJC.

• The creation of wider venues for fuller discussion of major challenges facing Jewish life:

We indicated elsewhere that the American desire for civility and politeness often mistakenly masks the reality that diverse, passionately-held positions exist on virtually every issue in Jewish life. Within American Jewry, there are contested views around such issues as patrilineal descent and its consequences, the place of Jewish gays and lesbians, same-sex marriage, and attitudes towards abortion. Clearly, except among the fervently Orthodox, there is no one Jewish answer. Debate takes place daily in our press, even on our streets, within our synagogues, and in a multiplicity of other venues associated with Jewish life. In our opinion, the Jewish community is strengthened when robust opinions are shared and when open dialogue is nurtured. The result ultimately will be a stronger community and a commitment to those values that bind us as a people.

Driven by the legitimate need to raise significant funds, the UJC and federations seek to avoid counterproductive divisiveness, desiring instead to achieve consensus. This aversion to engaging in intense debate needs to be challenged. Those who are the most passionate about Jewish causes and hold positions contrary to the "Jewish establishment" are frequently lost to the community.

Federations often do not represent the rich diversity of views that defines our communities. We do not believe the UJC must take stands which would split the communities, but we believe strongly that the federations and the UJC must provide venues to explore publicly the diverse views expressed within the community. This leads to our next set of recommendations.

4.    **Introduce Ways to Strengthen the Federation System:**

Many respondents pointed out the existence of an "old boy" network in Jewish life. This has resulted in blocking a broader cross section of leadership, especially the frequent and glaring under-representation of women. In addition to the plea to open the UJC to women, a similar call was made to recruit and advance numbers of younger people. Many felt that the focus on wealth as a dominant criterion for advancement in the communal system resulted in an increasingly non-representative body at the leadership level. The absence of other voices diminishes the UJC's role as a change agent within the federation system. The roadmap for change and for remaking the UJC begins at the bottom of an organization. This is where leaders engage not only the opinion makers and great thinkers of our time but also the citizens on the street. They are the people who we also want to support the community enterprise. Their involvement at all levels would not only sanction institutional governance but might also endorse and validate innovative proposals.

The above-mentioned recommendations partially capture the ideas shared with us by "the visionaries." Most of them saw the merger as a missed opportunity to create a truly new organization, geared toward anticipating and responding to the issues facing Jews and Jewish life in the 21$^{st}$ century. There continue to be opportunities to revisit the vision. Additionally, almost all respondents saw the UJC as "a work in progress." This suggests openness to reviewing the mission and functions necessary to make the UJC an innovative, responsive, and more meaningful organization.

- Introducing alternate governance structures:

Independent of one another, a few visionaries suggested the establishment of a bi-cameral board for the UJC. The premise was the desire to engage the mega-givers conjointly with community and organizational representatives. The powers would be delineated so as to connect mega-givers in a serious way, recognizing that no major initiative could take place without their consent. A second branch of governance within the UJC (modeled after the British House of Commons or the House of Representatives in America) would have the same power, i.e., granting consent for the implementation of actions suggested by the "Upper House."

Serious consideration should be given to reshaping the UJC governance structure in this way. No great innovations in Jewish life can be implemented without the wisdom and consent of the mega-givers. This would in no way mute those with the energy and capacity to introduce innovation in Jewish life. The mega-givers would be encouraged to continue their welcomed attempts to create change or refocus the priorities of American Jewry. Simultaneously, other groups would be encouraged to do the same. For the UJC, this will result in the provision of more venues for change, with larger numbers supporting and initiating changes themselves.

- Constructing a different model of national involvement:

For decades, the White House has initiated a grass-roots process for identifying concerns. Such White House-sponsored initiatives begin at the local level. These are followed by meetings at the regional and national level, which successively narrow recommendations and proposals for policy consideration. The outcome is an inclusive commitment to act on these shared ideas. To date, in Jewish life no such approach has been attempted. The UJC ought to be that venue. It could provide real opportunities for input from specialists and all others interested in helping to evolve a truly new Jewish agenda while confirming continuing needs and services, grounded in our history and tradition. The Orthodox community has steadily involved increasing numbers of Jews, encouraging individuals and groups to study one page of Talmud each day and in turn celebrating the completion of the study process with regular assemblies. The UJC could set into motion a comparable process geared to the critical communal issues of our times.

The Wexner Foundation's ambitious initiative to develop a cadre of lay and professional leaders for tomorrow represents an example of cooperation with existing Jewish institutions. The expenditure of tens of millions of dollars confirms the reality that appropriate visions can result in creative and revolutionary programs that can impact and alter Jewish life. The various initiatives of the Bronfmans, the Mandels, Shustermans, and Steinhardts, among others, actuate programs on a scale never before contemplated in Jewish history, which further confirms this premise.

The wedding of financial resources, innovative thinking, and risk-taking by these mega-givers needs a more formal and continuing connection to organized Jewish life. The foundations of these major donors have engaged an extraordinary cadre of professionals to design and implement programs and models of community building, often outside the mainstream communal infrastructure. This body of professionals also should be seen as an important resource, serving as an informal consulting body to UJC personnel, in addition to advising and consulting with Jewish researchers and think tanks.

## 5. Provide opportunities to debate, discuss, and react to Israel's policies:

The interviews in this study confirmed that the Israel agenda was not a matter of major concern to many respondents. While  support for Israel was indeed widespread, most American Jews, including some elements of its leadership, shied away from any public discourse and action about issues or concerns which departed from the Israel government's position.

There is at least one instance when the federation system organized itself to publicly contest a decision of the Israeli government. This occurred nearly twenty years ago when the government seemed poised to change the definition of "Who is a Jew" that had governed Israeli policy since the founding of the State. For purposes of *aliyah*, Prime Minister David Ben Gurion had declared, anyone with one Jewish grandparent would be considered "Jewish" by the State of Israel. Ben Gurion deliberately echoed, and stood on its head, the racial standards of the Third Reich. He felt strongly that this was a way of celebrating the triumph of Jewish continuity over racist, Nazis ideology.

When the controversy over the definition of "Who is a Jew" re-emerged in the late 1980s in Israel, American Jewish national organizations, secular and religious, sprang into action. Powerful lay representatives were sent to meet with Israel's president, prime minister, cabinet ministers and Knesset members to protest any decision to change the existing standard. On the other side, Orthodox groups sent their own representatives calling for a redefinition of "Who is a Jew" on Halachic grounds. In the end, all the voices of world Jewry were heard. The fear most frequently voiced was that, if the State reversed the existing understanding, support for Israel by American Jews would evaporate, and the sense of Jewish unity would be shattered. Ultimately, the proposal was withdrawn. No negative consequences resulted in the relationships between the two communities.

The propensity to silence public discourse in the North American community confuses the act of providing support for the State of Israel with the (arguable) necessity of supporting whichever political elite is in power. It ignores the strong differences within the American Jewish community as to the efficacy of that approach. At times, this unquestioning support has been in opposition to the policies and views of the American government and indeed the privately held opinions of many, if not most, American Jews. The rationale has been that a public show of unity by Jews in the United States will result in more support for Israel.. Where there are contentious issues that demand attention, the UJC might serve as the convener to stimulate and aid others organizations to take part in deliberations; in other instances, it might develop such opportunities itself. There is no mandate given to the UJC to be THE voice of American Jewry, but it has a responsibility to be a significant facilitator, shining light on issues of deep concern to American and indeed world Jewry. The great issues of the Jewish people need to be discussed and debated within the community and by the UJC. Its constituents on the local scene should provide a similar venue for such a discourse beyond the board room and in the community.

**6. Construct relationships with other national organizations and explore the concept of "outsourcing" some services now offered by the UJC:**

Jewish life is notorious for celebrating its open nature. Any group on the local, national, or international level can perceive an unmet need and develop a niche by addressing it. The market decides its fate – did it serve its clients well? Did it address the problems it perceived? A number of organizations, old and new, have achieved varying levels of status and prestige in the pursuit of their missions. Some may be living in the glory days of yesteryear.. Others rise, peak and may eventually disappear. Men's Zionist organizations are a good example of this reality in Jewish life today.

The great bulk of today's successful Jewish organizations represent a panoply of services offered across a wide spectrum of approaches and ideologies. According to the *American Jewish Year Book*, there are over 330 national and American-based groups related to Israel and other activities abroad. They are a rich resource for the federation system. Creative thought should be given to outsourcing activities or roles on behalf of the federations, deputizing them to act in the name of the UJC and the Jewish people. Similarly, organizations within the community devoted to the cultural arts could be asked to build bridges of understanding and perhaps joint activity between the world of the UJC and the arena of the arts. The National Foundation for Jewish Culture, mandated to preserve and nurture the creation of Jewish culture in America, is the natural venue for the pursuit of this possibility. Institutional collaboration and outsourcing of this sort might result in more frequent sharing of talent, resources, and creative energy.

**7. Establish the office of ombudsperson with the power to examine and report governance, fiscal matters, and policy development within the UJC:**

It remains an anomaly that the very democratic values which drive so much of American life are often implemented so minimally in Jewish life. The UJC has a great opportunity to demonstrate that those values might be incorporated into Jewish communal practice. An ombudsperson would be a great beginning step in the process. An individual of great personal stature and credibility could play a remarkable role if charged with the responsibility of sitting in on key policy meetings as an observer, monitoring and interpreting fiscal reports, and explaining the processes by which decisions were rendered and carried forward. Such an individual could perform a variety of valuable and innovative functions, by serving as a confidential sounding board for staff and providing a systematic way to both report and interpret major developments to organizational constituencies and the larger Jewish public. This would encompass sharing specific findings, monitoring services, accessing the governance process, and evaluating institutional performance, along with providing recommendations pertaining to best practices.

JAFI has an inspector general who issues annual reports evaluating its structure and internal actions. A refinement of the functions of that position, with appropriate adaptations for the American context, would do much to increase and retain confidence in future actions of the UJC. This model, if adopted, could be utilized on the local level as well.

**8. Help underwrite think tanks and use them in sustained ways:**

The issues facing Jewish life require significant new research and the introduction of alternative and new policy options. A handful of think tanks devoted to studying and examining Jewish life exist in America. Some are free standing, yet others are affiliated with universities. They are seriously under-funded and, as a result, their findings are too seldom publicized and/or employed. Serious attention should be given to encouraging unfettered research, while funding these efforts at an adequate level. In turn, these centers of Jewish research could work together in more practical ways by coordinating their efforts and sharing their findings. A national research fund should be established to nurture these new initiatives. Opportunities for consultation between practitioners and researchers would provide a new synergy, resulting in more focused approaches to problem solving and to ever-changing priorities.

**9. Promote true creativity and innovation:**

The CJF, UJA, UIA of old were perceived by many as stuck in the "old ways" of doing business. Many respondents bemoaned the lack of truly innovative initiatives and were frustrated by the difficulty in effectuating change. Assessing the most innovative structural and programmatic developments of the last decade confirms that judgment. Mega-givers, operating outside of these traditional structures, have launched a number of new programs. Birthright, the program initiated to bring thousands of first time young Jewish visitors to Israel, is possibly the best known of these initiatives. Among other newly established philanthropic organizations, the New Israel Fund (NIF), whose budget has increased eighty-seven fold in its brief 25 years of operation, represented a response on the part of its founders and donors to create a "hands-on" giving approach, while also seeking to assist and partner with non-establishment institutions in Israel. The NIF, along with other institutions, have incorporated in their programs the input of Israelis in planning and implementing programs, minimizing the paternalistic approach which so often characterized philanthropic activities in the past.

Within federations, there are certain structural and programmatic realities that must be considered when looking to encourage innovation. Many of these have grown out of the perceived need when making allocations to achieve consensus and also maximize participation under the federation "giving" umbrella. Yet a growing numbers of federations have established locally controlled, innovative and creative programs in Israel, outside of JAFI or Partnership 2000. Increased fundraising has often been the result. Recognizing their value, these federations asked the UJC to take the lead in modeling for its constituents the development and implementation of experimental programming.

Incubator laboratories should be created in local communities and on the national level. An investment of this sort could provide opportunities to experiment with all manner of activities and programs geared to emerging needs, changing institutions, and the uses of new technologies. As we learn from the business world, not all experiments are successful. But without an expenditure of research and development funds, we may never uncover and confirm the myriad of new approaches necessary for the realization of the mission of the UJC and federations.

## LEADERSHIP AND TRAINING

No area in Jewish communal life may require more attention at this time than a renewed focus on the educational development of our current and future professionals and the continuing enrichment of our lay leadership. We focus our attention here on strategies for recruitment and training.

**10. Construct a new working model for lay and staff development by:**

- developing broader opportunities for ongoing lay and staff training:

The field is rife with reports regarding heightened levels of lay-staff tension. The number of executive personnel terminated has increased markedly. The appropriate push to use sound business principles in managing personnel is accompanied at the same time by poor business practices introduced in the name of efficiency. The results have oftentimes been brutal and devastating. Of course, there are those who deserve to be fired. However, it must be remembered that there are dignified, humane, and, importantly, Jewish ways in managing and terminating relationships.

Governing Jewish life is often an arcane art, grounded in a unique and specific organizational culture. The need to recognize this while also identifying and emphasizing the changing mission of boards and institutions is imperative. There is a corresponding challenge to refocus our energies in delineating and unpacking lay-staff collaborative relationships.

Increasingly, within our communal institutions board members are not coming up through the ranks. Rather, a significant percentage of new members are being parachuted onto boards with little or no educational and socializing opportunities as a prior condition to their selection. Correspondingly, over the decades, there has been a great expansion in the professional (or non-professional) backgrounds of those assuming positions within the communal system. We use the word "professional" here in a precise manner. Today, one finds executive staff that often does not hold degrees in Jewish communal service, accompanied by training in related social welfare and public policy fields. In fact, these individuals may be lawyers or accountants. They may also be last year's successful campaign chair or a board member who has been particularly successful in his/her business or professional life. In some settings, they have concluded that they can manage the community's "businesses" more effectively than staff with whom they had previously been working.

As a result, professional development programs are needed at all levels. They must be geared toward those newly arrived from non-traditional backgrounds and settings with little or no experience in Jewish life; for those individuals with prior experience who are assuming positions at different levels or within different institutional settings; and for former lay leaders who are able to "jump the line" in order to assume professional positions.

Those who are already in the field require ongoing opportunities to update themselves through exposure to cutting edge knowledge and practice. We must further enhance their competencies in studying organizational and management theory; interpreting new demographic data; acquiring Jewish knowledge; and mastering the latest in fund development strategies, and supervisory and evaluative practices. Presently there is no "certification process" outside of the clinical, medical, and rabbinical settings. Jewish institutional service increasingly demands such a standard of practice, since it represents a defined discipline. The same expectations ought to apply to federations, community relation agencies, community centers and other communal settings where no such standards currently exist.

Boards of directors often have no clear understanding of the role of the professional. For most, it is a simple differentiation between those who are paid and those who volunteer. Instead, the unique sets of skills, competencies, bodies of knowledge and values that define a professional should be developed to help delineate the two separate roles.

- working more closely with schools of Jewish communal service:

There needs to be a mechanism to evaluate and further develop agreed upon criteria and standards of professional service. At the same time, it is essential to develop a national fund to underwrite scholarships for students and to establish a national lay leadership-training center. (See appendix for historical background and the development of schools and programs of Jewish communal service.)

In 1951, the first fully accredited school of social work under Jewish auspices was developed by Yeshiva University (the Wurzweiler School of Social Work). It is still thriving. It did not perceive itself nor was it recognized as solely serving the Jewish community. Yet a substantial number of its graduates have served in Jewish communal settings. In 1968, Hebrew Union College and Brandeis University established programs solely devoted to Jewish communal service. There are now ten such programs. They have often attempted, sometimes together and sometimes independently, to construct a body of knowledge, skills, methods and values, which are the attributes of a profession.

Over the years, more than 1500 people have earned degrees in the communal service programs. The quality of the students may vary, but research and anecdotal reports indicate that a significant number of these graduates have risen to high posts in American Jewish life. Regrettably, the very communal system that they

107

serve has provided almost no serious funding in support of their education.

It should be clear that this initiative to create a body of trained communal professionals involved a century long effort. The lack of sufficient resources helps explain the demise of many of these earlier programs (see Appendix V). Similarly, the absence of ongoing coordination and interaction between "town and gown" also represents a major reason for the collapse of these earlier educational initiatives. Reflecting changes in attitude, the programs that have existed since the 1960s have enjoyed greater economic viability.

The schools, while more economically sustainable than in the past, are still under funded by the communal system. Given the high cost of graduate professional education, the gap between the field and the programs remains a topic of ongoing concern. Standards of practice and the field's expectations of its graduates need to be clarified.

The talents and energies of the students and faculty remain both under valued and under utilized. Pressing communal needs might be brought to the schools of Jewish communal service. For example, faculty from one or more of these professional schools might be recruited to help guide future training programs involving lay leadership. By virtue of their training and experience, these men and women are uniquely sensitive to the realities of Jewish organizational cultures.

The post World War II and 1950s generation of professional leadership is now leaving the scene. To supplant the accumulated wisdom and experience of these individuals, the best and the brightest must be recruited to work in Jewish communal settings. It is imperative that the number and dollar amount of available scholarships be dramatically increased. After all, most graduates who go into the field are already saddled with college loan debt between ten and forty thousand dollars. With starting annual salaries ranging from thirty-five to fifty thousand dollars, many young professionals find themselves struggling either to stay in the field or meet their obligations. Moreover, given the salary scale in the field, relatively few young professionals can afford the very services they often bring to the community – education, camping, synagogue, and JCC memberships.

To the credit of selected generous mega-givers, some steps have already been taken to mitigate the loan burden and expand the scholarship pool. More is needed to assure that the best students enter the field and to enhance the attractiveness of the profession. Additionally, the great – and growing – gap between beginning salaries and senior staff salaries must be addressed. Entry-level rabbis (who admittedly spend more years studying than a graduate communal service student) receive salaries that are on average twice that of a beginning communal professional. However, while a senior rabbi will earn two to three times more than a recently-ordained rabbi, in the Jewish communal field, senior staff salaries are often as much as six times that of an entry level professional. We do not decry the salaries earned by senior executives; we believe, however, that the differential is too great. More equity at the entry levels is required to attract and retain the most desirable and committed individuals to the field.

• National Training Center for Lay Leadership

The Sherman Leadership Seminars at Brandeis University have influenced a significant number of lay leaders over the years owing to the visionary efforts of Bernard Reisman. The model is a good one but limited in nature by virtue of time constraints. Serious attention must be given to helping lay leadership set aside time to study and learn more than before. A curriculum, which includes Jewish history, sociology and texts along with an exposure to the structure of Jewish governance, here and abroad, is essential.

109

Along with nonprofit governance principles, lay leaders must have and continue to develop insights into management practices related to role delineation and board-staff relations. Joint training opportunities for board and staff members would add immeasurably to building the seamless leadership teams that are required to lead and manage our federations. We are certain that the schools and programs of Jewish communal service would aid in that process.

**11. Focus on a balanced division of power between lay and professional leadership, while creating broader opportunities for lay and professional training:**

It was clear from our interviews that a majority of people felt that the professionals were the most active group in the merger deliberations. Implied or voiced among the visionaries was the notion that, in the delicate balance of lay-staff relations, a disproportionate amount of power had shifted to the professionals.

This seems to be a consequence of the adoption in recent years of a corporate model as the norm in federation governance. The evolving transition of titles from the nonprofit sector (where agencies used to be led by executive directors) to the nomenclature of the for-profit sector (where the top slot is held by the president and chief executive officer) confirms this new reality. Under this model the visioning and managing of the corporate mission has tilted to the office of the president, that is, the professional. The result has been an increased centralization of control.

Board function has also been truncated, if not diminished in this new model. In many instances, the very process of choosing (the smaller and small number of) board members is in the hands of, or heavily influenced by, the president or CEO. Where this new reality exists, there is a need to restore balance. A substantial number of lay respondents commented on the centralizing of power within the UJC as a result of the merger. They pointed out that far fewer lay leaders were involved than before, and more than a few lay leaders felt they had been dropped or driven away from important governance roles. While seeking to achieve operational efficiencies, this group wanted to create a better synthesis between the traditional governance model and the current power-centered, corporate approach. It is important to note that the bulk of the respondents are themselves products of the best of corporate thinking and practice in their private roles.

All of this requires a commitment to consultation and collaboration by both lay leaders and professionals. All must understand that they are not only building institutions but they are also creating learning environments. A significant investment must be made in the lay-professional relationship. If the communal enterprise is to flourish, there must be serious attention paid to the ongoing training of our professionals. Similarly, there must be a willingness on the part of lay leaders to pursue a path of inquiry where they will study both Jewish texts as well as organizational and management practice. Today, organizational participants, lay and professional, must see themselves as learners; such engagement is essential for both institutional growth and effectiveness.

# *CLOSING WORDS*

We hope we captured the central elements related to the process of creating the UJC, along with identifying key themes connected to representation and inclusion. This merger process was a test of the players and their roles. It was about federation professionals seeking to reconstruct a system that they believe required institutional re-engineering. This was also about the egos and passions of lay leaders surrendering positions and giving up institutional loyalties in order to construct a new communal framework. It was necessary, according to one respondent, that everyone "be equally discomforted" and that may have indeed occurred. The lessons learned among the participants varied. Some tended to regret the merger outcome, feeling the process had not evolved as desired. Some regretted the mix of participants, namely, the use of outside consultants, "outside" lay leaders, and the role of professionals. But in the end, as throughout history, the Jewish people and its institutions will reflect our authentic voice.

Our findings confirmed for us that we had successfully interviewed most of the people who over the years had been involved in the seven years of discussion leading to merger. Through the classifications we employed, we were able to differentiate the varied and thoughtful perspectives of these key stakeholders. As noted, people acknowledged "winners" and "losers" associated with this process. Our hope would be that the ultimate portrait of the UJC would reflect the creativity, wisdom and leadership that has so richly defined our community and shaped its institutions. The end result was a new organization, which met few if anyone's expectations. Many described it as "a work in progress," yet serious questions remain regarding its status. One of our respondents stated: "Nobody got it right. We could simply not be able to do it at this time".

Some envisioned the possibility of constructing a radically new kind of national institution that would play a much more comprehensive role in Jewish life, addressing the priorities facing a changing American Jewish community. Such an institutional voice of the Jewish people would creatively address the issues of education, assimilation, representation to the greater society, and the development of new thinking around the Israel-Diaspora connection. For them, serious attention would be given as well to redefining the concept of "collective responsibility" and the roles of local federations in coming together to deal with emergent and ongoing issues in a coordinated approach.

We believe that in the course of this process, much learning occurred; yet more will be needed in order for the UJC to emerge as an institution that can ultimately serve the Jewish people in this new century. It is our hope that communal leadership will be stimulated to think and act upon our recommendations along with other ideas and proposals which may arise. Inevitably, the fears and expectations of the blending of three organizational cultures and integrating diverse leadership styles and visions will define the outcome of this merger. The challenge will be to respond to the needs of the present and the dreams of the future, while functioning within budgetary restraints and organizational realities. The baby has been born. How will it be raised, and what awaits us, depends on the parenting it will receive in the decade ahead.

## *QUESTIONS ASKED IN THIS STUDY:*

The participants were asked to respond to the 11 interview questions listed here:

1. What brought about the merger of UIA, UJA, and CJF?

2. Were you in agreement with the idea of merger?

3. Did any one of the organizations involved in the merger benefit more than the others?

4. Would you have preferred a different model than the present one? What would it have been?

5. Who were those most active in the merger process?

6. Did professionals play roles disproportionate to their authority?

7. Did people from any particular organization seem to dominate the merger efforts?

8. Were you satisfied with the final outcome?

9. Did you feel the process, which produced the merged organization, a representative one?

10. Were there any "winners" and "losers"? Who were they?

11. What general lessons did you learn from the merger process?

# APPENDIX I – LIST OF RESPONDENTS

The authors warmly acknowledge those who agreed to be interviewed. Without their open and full cooperation this study would not have been possible.

1. Bennett Aaron* **, Philadelphia, PA
2. Caryn Adelman, Chicago, IL
3. Daniel Allen, Hartford, CT
4. Sam Asher*, St. Paul, MN
5. Lionel Bell*, Los Angeles, CA
6. Paul Berger* **, Washington, DC
7. Mel Bloom, New York, NY
8. Charles Bronfman, New York, NY
9. Shoshana S. Cardin**, Baltimore, MD
10. Stanley Chesley*, Cincinnati, OH
11. Ted Farber, Rockville, MD
12. Irwin Field**, Los Angeles, CA
13. Lawrence W. Fine*, Rochester, NY
14. John Fishel, Los Angeles, CA
15. Darryl Friedman, Baltimore, MD
16. Conrad Giles* **, Detroit, MI
17. Herb Glaser, Los Angeles, CA
18. Robert Goldberg*, Cleveland, OH
19. Charles R. Goodman*, Chicago, IL
20. Nancy Grand, San Francisco, CA
21. Alexander Grass**, Harrisburg, PA
22. Barbara Himmelrich*, Baltimore, MD
23. Stephen Hoffman*, Cleveland, OH
24. Stanley Horowitz, New York, NY
25. Alan Jaffe* **, New York, NY
26. Joseph Kanfer* **, Akron, OH
27. Dick Katz*, San Diego, CA
28. Jeffrey L. Klein*, Palm Beach, FL
29. Max L. Kleinman, Whippany, NJ
30. Jonathan W. Kolker* **, Baltimore, MD

31. Martin Kraar, New York, NY
32. Doron Krakow, New York, NY
33. Marvin Lender* **, New Haven, CT
34. Joan Levin* **, Jacksonville, FL
35. Irwin Levy, West Palm Beach, FL
36. Brian Lurie, San Francisco, CA
37. Herman Markowitz, Minneapolis, MN
38. Bernard Moscovitz, New York, NY
39. Neil Moss*, Columbus, OH
40. Robert Naftaly*, Detroit, MI
41. Steve Nasatir*, Chicago, IL
42. Rebecca Newman * **, San Diego, CA
43. David Nussbaum, Deal, NJ
44. Richard L. Pearlstone**, Baltimore, MD
45. Judith Stern Peck*, New York, NY
46. Marlene Post, New York, NY
47. Albert Ratner * **, Cleveland, OH
48. Howard Reiger*, Pittsburgh, PA
49. Barry Rosenberg*, St. Louis, MO
50. Naomi Rosenfeld*, Ft. Worth, TX
51. Howard Ross, Shreveport, LA
52. Michael Rukin, Boston, MA
53. John Ruskay, New York, NY
54. Melvin Salberg**, New York, NY
55. Jay I. Sarver, St. Louis, MO
56. Ivan Michael Schaeffer*, Washington, DC
57. Charles Schiffman, Portland, OR
58. Michael Schneider, New York, NY
59. Miriam A. Schneirov**, Philadelphia, PA
60. Carmi Schwartz, New York, NY
61. Jodi Schwartz* **, New York, NY
62. Jane Sherman**, Detroit, MI
63. Barry Shrage, Boston, MA
64. Alan Shulman**, Miami, FL
65. Robert Silverman*, Springfield, IL
66. Nancy Siwak*, St. Louis, MO

67. Sanford Solender, deceased
68. Stephen Solender, New York, NY
69. Carole A. Soloman* **, New York, NY
70. Jeffrey Solomon, New York, NY
71. Joel Tauber* **, Detroit, MI
72. Andrew Tisch*, New York, NY
73. Jacques Torczyner, Walnut Creek, CA
74. John Uhlmann*, Kansas City, MO
75. Andrea Weinstein*, Dallas, TX
76. Gary Weinstein*, Dallas, TX
77. Howard Weisband, Jerusalem, Israel
78. Richard Wexler*, Chicago, IL
79. Maynard Wishner**, Chicago, IL
80. Jay Yoskowitz, New York, NY
81. Eric Yoffie, New York, NY

seven anonymous respondents

*Cities listed were at the time of the merger for those who served on committees*

- • * Served on Drafting Committee for the New Entity, 1998
- • ** Served on the Joint Operating Committee, 1998

# APPENDIX II – NATIONAL CONSULTATION ON THE UJC STUDY

*February 2, 2005*

The authors of this study convened a consultation in New York on February 2nd attended by 24 people, most of whom had been participants in our interview process. The individuals present included past and present national Jewish leaders encompassing all of the primary institutions associated with the merger process, community representatives including federation professionals and lay leaders, foundation officials, rabbis, and academics. We saw this as an opportunity to garner feedback from a representative group of UJC stakeholders regarding our findings and the recommendations that we offered as a result of our study.

Outside of a few introductory comments, as authors of this study, we purposely conceived our role for this day to be that of observers. As a result, we invited one of our colleagues, Dr. Carl Sheingold, President of the Reconstructionist Jewish Federation and a former senior professional officer of the Council of Jewish Federations, to facilitate the discussion.

The design of the day enabled those present to react to the content, conclusions, and recommendations of our study. As with our study, the comments and reflections offered at this consultation are presented without attribution.

## Reflections of on "Predictability to Chaos??," the Study

Most of the consultation addressed specific themes found both within the study or more generally referenced the workings of the UJC during its early years of operation. A few comments were specifically directed to the format and focus of the document itself. Several individuals reiterated what we had attempted to note in the study that this report represented two structural realities: it was a snapshot in time and it reflected the reactions of those we interviewed.

Commenting on the title of the study, one person observed that "there is no virtue in 'predictability'." And similarly, in light of the interest currently in chaos theory, 'chaos' ought not be seen as necessarily something to be avoided but rather offers the observer "different patterns in understanding the flow of events."

One participant argued that it was "not so clear" as the study seemed to suggest who were the true "winners and losers" in this process. While others were concerned that the issues associated with the mission and vision of the UJC did not seem to enter into the discussions with our interviewees. More details associated with the UJC mission are introduced below.

This was seen by one respondent as a study on the "process" of creating the UJC as against a review of the "content" pertaining to its organizational purpose or mission. Another felt that just as UJC has not successfully engaged the smaller communities, the concerns of these federations were "lost in the document".

In seeking to capture the input we received, we have summarized the daylong discussions around five core themes.

1. Focusing on Structural and Governance Concerns
2. Revisiting the Mission and Vision of UJC
3. Defining UJC: Trade Association vs. New Voice for American Jewry
4. Considering the Recommendations
5. Identifying New Opportunities

In revisiting the merger negotiations, a number of the consultation participants acknowledged the "human failures" associated with the final product, where mistakes were made in constructing the new entity. Paraphrasing Mel Brooks, one participant concluded: "Where did we go right?" Similarly, they concluded that this experience must be seen as a unique moment, but no similar or transferable experiences upon which to draw.

**Focusing on Structural and Governance Concerns**:

In reviewing the structural and procedural concerns associated with the merger, the discussion touched upon <u>seven</u> principal themes:

## 1. Learning Curves

Several respondents acknowledged the complexities and challenges faced in crafting a new national instrument for the Jewish people. They readily noted that "we had unrealistic expectations", "made lots of mistakes", and "experienced disappointments"

We might, as one participant offered, try to employ the Quakers' definition of consensus: "as everybody moving on in order to try something different, even if they don't agree on the particular outcome."

According to one participant, the system contains a series of built-in "fatal flaws" including whether or not collective responsibility was a widely accepted principle, changing lay leadership, and the independence of local federations. As a result, the UJC will need to develop alternative ways to move key national initiatives forward as a way to galvanize federations and over come some of these impediments (some of the specific ideas are introduced in later sections of this report). In this process, according to one source, we "replicated the old while not taking into account new needs."

As one person noted, UJC required a period of "stabilization" and may now be in a position to move forward. Some noted that UJC is not about the "alignment of the Jewish people" but rather about bringing the federation system together. In addition, national organizations face significantly different challenges than do local institutions. They need to be accountable to the varying demands of their multiple constituencies.

The discussion around organizational cultural differences among the merging institutions also introduced a broader reference to the more significant cultural and organizational differences within the Jewish world between federations and the religious and Zionist organizations. Similarly, one needed to understand the unique cultural features that defined the foundation world and academia if the UJC were to enter into a working relationship with these different constituencies.

As one participant concluded, "There are no mergers, only takeovers." Another concluded, "Change is both hard and painful."

## 2. UJA Brand Name

A number of individuals addressed this item, with most acknowledging that a mistake may have been made in not retaining the "UJA" label. Several participants suggested that the merger team had been advised by outside consultants, experts on consumer matters, to abandon the UJA name as a way of attracting younger and newer donors. One individual commented that not taking on the UJA name must be seen as "not acting responsibly." Yet others found the debate over the name change as not significant to the overall operational success of the UJC. These individuals argued that it is the quality of the product that UJC will create that in the end will define its credibility and effectiveness rather than the "brand name," itself.

## 3. Religious Streams and the Zionist Movement

The question of how and whether to include the religious movements and the Zionist organizations came up in various contexts. A number of individuals reflected on how this matter was dealt with in the merger negotiations. For some, the question of constructing a truly "visionary instrument" for the transformation of Jewish life would have by necessity involved the inclusion of these groups within any new national institution. One person in addressing this idea commented that religion represents a "central aspect of American society" and that Judaism must be seen as a "fundamental determinant of Jewish identity."

Some suggested that the system of constructing "pillars" was designed to allow for these voices to participate actively in the substantive agenda of the UJC. Outside of one seat that would be reserved on the Executive Committee for the religious streams, the general thinking was to encourage the religious and Zionist representatives to see their local federations and the four UJC pillars as the appropriate venues for their institutional engagement with the federation system.

Clearly, the current UJC governance model failed to create a fundamentally new national institution providing representation to these significant national constituencies, which in the end angered the leadership of the religious streams and Zionist representatives.

### 4. "The Gender Thing" and Other Missing Ingredients

One person specifically noted the relative absence of women in the study and the corresponding non-presence of women in executive positions of the large-city federations and within the ranks of lay leadership as well.

Similar concerns were offered with reference to the concerns and interests of the intermediate and small city federations who were "lost in the document."

## 5. Lessons from Other Mergers

A number of individuals referred to community-based and religious institutional mergers as a way of extracting learning curves for the UJC experience. While it was possible to extract some generic principles from these other case studies, a general assessment seemed to suggest that it was not possible to transfer these experiences to the institutional complexities and cultural ingredients associated with the formation of a new national organization.

In reading the data from the study, one individual suggested that the language of merger used "commercial" language rather than reflecting the Jewish character to this process.

## 6. Collective Responsibility

One of the factors associated with the perceived failure of the UJC was the issue of "collective responsibility". The success of UJC was seen as directly tied to the buy-in by member federations of their financial obligations to meet specific expectations laid out by the national system. Those present in our consultation felt that the unwillingness of federations to fully accept obligations of collective responsibility fundamentally undermined the ability of UJC to succeed with its core mission. Some who challenged this notion argued that individual federations had different perspectives on shaping a shared national and international agenda. Where limited consensus appeared today to be operative within this communal structure, it was not possible to impose or expect a collective buy-in from federations.

## 7. Lay and Professional Leadership

Respondents in our survey addressed lay-professional relationships in detail. Those participating in our consultation did not see the same levels of tension between these two sectors but rather felt that professionals were constructive and supportive of the process. Several expressed specific concerns about the engagement and quality of lay leadership participation. One person observed: "Where were the lay leaders?" Another individual suggested that "there was great respect and good engagement" among the participants in the process. This person went on to suggest "Everyone was committed "to doing the right thing."

One individual noted that he had heard some federation executives refer to "owning the system", a frequently utilized term referenced in our study as well.

Elsewhere in this report, we list the specific recommendations associated with the preparation and training of lay and professional leaders.

**Revisiting the Mission and Vision Themes of the UJC**

A significant number of the respondents perceived an absence of discussion among those interviewed for the study and their understanding of the place of mission and vision within the merger negotiations. Many of our participants were uniformly disappointed in the absence of any serious discussion within this study of the centrality of documents related to the mission and vision of a merged organization in helping to shape and guide both the process and the outcome.

One person suggested that, "we effectuated the merger for the wrong reasons". The implementation process "ignored the reasons for it." Referring to a comment from the study that "we took the extraordinary and made it ordinary", this individual concluded that it is "our responsibility today to make UJC extraordinary".

124

In trying to examine the question of mission and vision, one participant suggested that national organizations in particular have a difficult time to convey their mission, often being removed from their constituencies by distance and time. As a result a series of competing expectations seem to emerge: collective responsibility versus local autonomy; unity in conflict with representativeness; and quick decisions as against a discourse where all points of view are expressed and represented.

### Defining UJC: Trade Association vs. New Voice for American Jewry

One of the daunting questions that was asked throughout the day, can UJC somehow serve two masters? Is it able to both represent the interests and meet the needs of federations while also becoming a new institutional voice representing American Jewry?

As one participant asked, "What is wrong with a good trade association?" As the central address it can "advocate" on behalf of the interests of federations, create a "common language", construct a "shared agenda", "promote pride", and "encourage investing" in this system. "If people believe in this system it will work." "The big ideas come on their own." In the past communities have rallied around these concerns, and "we know people will respond."

Here one could not extract consensus as the discussion suggested that there were clearly divided sentiments. A core number of participants felt that UJC still needed to demonstrate its capacity to serve the federated system. As was noted by one individual, UJC represented a "pretense to reinvention". Smaller communities believed that the merger reflected a "missed opportunity" and the emergence of the UJC, in the opinion of one participant, did not represent "a darn bit of difference on how we operate."

One individual argued that "natural processes" would propel this system forward. Others however suggested that this was possibly "the right moment" to project a new vision for UJC.

For at least one person the question of mission remained open-ended. Would UJC emerge as a national problem-solving institution or in turn would it function as a trade association?

Some individuals reminded their colleagues that the federations "had pushed for merger," yet in the end there had emerged a battle involving the continued intent of some federations to press for "local sovereignty" which stood in conflict with UJC's attempt to construct a system that reflected the "will of the majority." This scenario, as described by one participant, involved a group of federations that were operating in "non-compliance" with the "owners of the UJC".

Some felt that now five years beyond creation, UJC could redefine its mission. Yet, others appeared less optimistic as both the process and the outcome were conceived of as a "missed opportunity". One person reported that when the name UJC was mentioned within some community settings, there appeared to be a level of "discomfort", a feeling that this entity is "not providing vision, cohesion, and broad unity."

Someone suggested that until federations accepted UJC as their "home", it would be premature to invite others into this system.

**Considering the Recommendations**

Eleven recommendations were introduced in the study. In the course of the discussions only several of these items were discussed in any significant detail. As noted elsewhere there was considerable comment offered around the restoration of the UJA name (Recommendation One). There were a few, mostly negative comments directed toward the second of our recommendations associated with UJC adopting a new national model of organizing similar to Big Brothers Big Sisters of America. Those who did offer input here noted how difficult it was to manage the current system with its highly individualized and nuanced federation participation with the current national system to expect a more centralized organizing approach. One person felt a "franchise" approach was totally inappropriate as a model. Again with the third of our recommendations, calling for wider venues for fuller representation and participation in Jewish life, there were some general comments pertaining to the role of academics. Several individuals questioned whether academics would have any interest in the policy making and management issues associated with this system, yet acknowledged that their talents as treasured community resources and as experts in specific areas ought to be incorporated with this system.

With the fifth of our recommendations to provide opportunities to debate, discuss, and react to Israel's policies, the general but limited comments offered suggested that such discussions ought to occur through the pillars or at the communal level. In connection with the sixth proposition, "constructing relationships with other national organizations and exploring the concept of 'outsourcing' some services now offered by UJC," we received only one comment that acknowledged that such outsourcing was already being employed.

The seventh recommendation, which called upon UJC to establish an ombudsperson office drew two specific comments. One respondent questioned the purpose for such an a function while the second individual felt that Chief Financial Officer already played such a role within UJC. Both recommendations eight (underwrite and employ think tanks) and nine (promote true creativity and innovation) were only indirectly dealt with during our consultation. One participant urged that UJC fulfill organizational functions that local federations are not able to perform. In connection with these two recommendations, the extensive discussion on the Trust for

Jewish Philanthropy, which is considered elsewhere in this document, seems to align with these principles.

The last two recommendations, which focus on "Leadership and Training," received minimal notice. The first of these called for a "new working model for lay and staff development" and provided a number of specific suggestions for collaborative and innovative training. The last of the recommendations (number eleven) addressed the question of insuring a "balance of power between lay and professional leadership." This later item, while reviewed elsewhere in the context of the discussion on the merger process, was not addressed as part of the recommendations of the study.

In examining the outcomes of the merger process, one respondent acknowledged the absence in both quantity and quality of lay leadership to both construct this new model and to effectively lead the enterprise. Another person noted that one of the continuing dilemmas associated with building a cadre of engaged lay leaders was the rapid turn around time of their service as key officers and presidents of their federations.

Two participants acknowledged the critical need within the federation system for professional recruitment and training. One spoke to the general issue of focusing key resources on both preparing professionals and lay leaders to assume the demands of communal and national leadership. A reference was offered to the role of the national system and to foundations in providing the type and scope of training needed by our communal systems and religious institutions. A foundation representative noted that graduates from various training programs for lay and professionals were not being fully utilized by the system as educators and resource persons.

# APPENDIX III – IDENTIFYING NEW OPPORTUNITIES

## Coalition of the Willing and the Trust for Jewish Philanthropy

A number of individuals focused on the need for a process to rethink the big ideas. But in shaping a new agenda this may in part require a new coalition of players that might include a different constellation of players for specific broad national initiatives. The list of critical participants included mega donors, foundations, academics, rabbis and religious institutions and federations.

The ideas were sweeping and significant. Several coined the idea of a "coalition of the willing" while others referenced the need to revitalize the Trust for Jewish Philanthropy. Still others embraced the expressed concept of a second chamber as called for in the recommendations that might represent the interests of Jewish funders, or some other mechanism for broad-based action and for mounting special campaigns to achieve new outcomes. Several saw this renewed focus on special funding initiatives as a way to engage the smaller federations which are not equipped to sustain and manage endowment programs. Commenting on the Trust, several representatives described its demise as a "strategic error."

Individuals identified a number of specific areas that might be "building blocks" for such shared initiatives. Individuals proposed that different sets of coalition players and funders would need to be organized around specific domestic and international agenda items. A number of areas were introduced as possible priority concerns; these included: (1) poverty programs to be responsive to the safety net concerns within Israel; (2) the Ethiopian National Project; and (3) early Jewish child care programs accompanied by a voucher plan underwriting those in need. Drawing from the experiences of such programs as Birthright Israel and Partnership 2000 and other case studies, such as the Tsunami Relief Campaign, how might we construct programs that can be responsive to international,

national, and domestic priorities? In redesigning this idea of a Trust or national funding program, some argued that both federations and groups outside of the federated system should be able to offer proposals and compete for resources under this model.

One participant inquired if this wasn't the time to revisit introducing the "domestic needs assessment" proposal as a way to prioritize communal priorities. As Americans think and act in a local context and where local control is paramount, a renewed focus on domestic concerns might be particularly appealing.

**Professional Education Initiatives**

One individual raised the question of whether UJC together with the seminaries might construct some type of "sustained system of involvement" in the training and orientation of future rabbis and educators about the communal system, as they would be better able to become powerful and supportive allies to the communal world.

Several folks felt that the unique role for the UJC would be in such areas as research and development and more directly to create training programs for communal professionals in conjunction with key funders, such as Wexner and Mandel, and with academic institutions already engaged in such an enterprise. One individual proposed that by bringing together foundations, the federation system, the existing professional training programs, and possibly the government, it might be possible to construct a one hundred million dollar fund to help train a new generation of Jewish communal professionals.

Another responded argued that we were not effectively engaging the alumni of existing training programs, both lay persons and professionals, as resource persons in our efforts to train and educate others.

## International and Israel-Based Organizations and Programs

The expanded fund-raising roles of JDC and the Jewish Agency in the American "market place" was noted. Discussion turned to the extent UJC and local federations might or should be involved in trying to coordinate these efforts.

One discussant suggested that in light of the significant number of Israel-based institutions and charities now active in this country, how UJC might help to work with these organizations and assist in coordinating their presence on the American scene

Others addressed the idea that UJC had failed to date to be the bridge in building stronger connections on all levels between Israel and North American Jewry and this ought to be one of the core functions of such a structure.

Aligned with both earlier comments related to new initiatives, one individual proposed that an "assembly of the Jewish people" be convened that would bring the Partnership communities together, both from Israel and the Diaspora, to explore shared issues around poverty concerns and community building issues. The Jewish Agency's best product and primary asset is Partnership 2000, and this would provide an interesting opportunity to study and act on a shared agenda.

One respondent suggested that the UJC should begin to partner with Israel's major philanthropists in addressing the social gap crisis within the country and become involved in providing programs that encourage and promote conversion among Russians and Ethiopians. Such initiatives might be convened jointly with the government, outside funders, and the federations.

## Changing Governance of the UJC

The consultation was informed of a number of new initiatives under the current UJC administration. Among the items under consideration involved a different governance model as well as institutional accountability measures that would be designed to assess outcomes and establish goals or targets, along with constructing "a pro-active culture."

## Closing Notions

Others spoke more generically believing that it is "not too late to change the environment and bring about healing," "to create a new dynamic," and "to change the culture." In referencing the issues of institutional culture, one respondent felt that the task of blending the fundraisers with the program people within the UJC system still required attention.

Some of those present challenged current UJC officials to broaden the avenues of partnership with foundations, academic centers, and other national and even international resources.

In the end some suggested, as noted elsewhere in these notes, that UJC would ultimately need to decide whether it would be defining itself as a "closed system" of federations or a more open one embracing the issues and institutions that comprised the broader Jewish scene.

## CONFERENCE ATTENDEES:

Aaron, Bennett
Allen, Daniel
Bubis, Gerald
Chazan, Cindy
Ellenson, David
Fine, Lawrence
Gottschalk, Alfred
Heller, Zachery
Katz, Roshelle
Kleinman, Max
Lender, Marvin
Mintz Geffen, Rela
Nasatir, Steve
Rieger, Howard
Rosen Adelman, Caryn
Salberg, Melvin
Saxe, Leonard
Sheingold, Carl
Shrage, Barry
Tauber, Joel
Wexler, Richard
Windmueller, Steven

# APPENDIX IV – THE LITERATURE ON MERGERS AND COLLABORATION

## Looking at Institutional Realignment:

There is a growing body of literature devoted to an examination of mergers and collaborative initiatives within the nonprofit sector. Many of the key elements associated with the creation of the UJC are apparent within such publications.

A central concept in the literature on organizational development deals with institutional realignment. As institutions of all types seek to achieve operational efficiency, manage consumer expectations, and deliver effective services and programs, organizational leaders employ various tools designed to introduce and manage change process.

To understand the process, one must begin with a set of key principles taken from the literature on organizational behavior and change management. The first of these involves tracking an institution's performance to understand its successes and weaknesses. Much of this tracking process includes monitoring other successful institutions in order to learn how they work, while seeking to identify their core competencies.

Secondly, organizations should replicate their successes rather than focus on fixing their failures. Scholars, such as Peter Drucker, suggest that asking the right questions is often the key to success in business. The same can be said of nonprofit institutions. Five core questions should be considered: "What's already working? Why is it working? What is the objective? What are the benefits? What can we do more of, or better, to achieve the objective?"

So where does institutional realignment occur? The literature on change management describes examples of incredible latitude.

Change can begin either inside or outside of an organization. Furthermore, change often has no identifiable constituency. As a result, key stakeholders, primary donors, and members, by their behavior and words, define what they expect or need from organizations without prior sanction for changing the very organizations they represent. Sometimes the pressure for change comes from a constituency. It becomes the task of the leaders to give the form and substance to life which responds to those pressures. From there it becomes the task of institutional leaders to manage the change process. According to Oakley (1994), when making change, institutional leaders must consider how to:

- produce real change, not merely rhetorical change;
- identify in advance the possible roadblocks and be prepared to deal with these challenges; and,
- know an organization's journey, i.e. its culture and the context of how an institution has operated, in order to understand the impact of change on primary constituencies.

Organizational learning, a facet of organizational behavior, is "not simply the sum of what all the members of an organization know; rather, it is the collective use of their capability to make sense of the world. In this context, learning is a verb, not a noun. It is not knowledge that is stored but the process that creates knowledge." For example, organizational learning does not take place without individual learning. Specific decision-makers are key elements in introducing and implementing the change process. "Organizational learning leads to continuous change in institutions and not simply to one-time transitions. Finally, organizational learning is the foe of those who would manage and the ally of those who would lead"(Dixon, 1995).

In the end, organizations reflect their leaders' style and practices. To change organizations, leaders must give their people the opportunity to change the ways in which they think and interact regarding the culture and performance of an institution (Dixon, 1995).

The second theme aligned with organizational behavior is change management. One model suggests that there are five stages to the change management process, and one must be aware of the dynamics throughout such transitions. As the idea of change often has negative connotations, institutional leaders must overcome levels of resistance in order to produce credible and effective results.

The ideas below refer to individual behaviors and collective responses during the five stages of institutional transition (Managers Edge, 1998):

1. *Denial:* Give people plenty of information.

2. *Anger:* Seek to listen and understand, praise and reward.

3. *Bargaining:* As some people seek to divert the process, redirect their energy and concerns toward the realities and benefits of change.

4. *Exploration:* Create short-term goals that produce victories, boost morale and provide opportunities for people to learn and grow.

5. *Commitment:* Secure buy-in from all participants by establishing a mission statement and shared goals.

The stages introduced here provide an overview of the change process. Extracted from business and organizational literature, these themes identify the core components related to the administration of change and have specific relevance, in our view, to an assessment of the merger process.

**The Ten Commandments of Change Management:**

1. Focus on the end product or service.

2. Maintain quality throughout the institution, even during periods of transition.

3. Remain market driven.

4. Customize your services, programs, and product.

5. Place your best people in settings where they directly impact your consumers.

6. Concentrate on what your institution does best.

7. Focus on team building, empowering people, and decentralizing certain functions.

8. Celebrate victories and always acknowledge your people.

9. Allow for experimentation and testing as a key to determining change strategies.

10. Everything in an institution can be changed, *except your core values.*

In the 21$^{st}$ century when organizations are constantly encountering environmental or external challenges and internal pressures, there are several key features of how institutions and even communities behave. In this era, it seems that all institutions are in constant transition. They are reinventing themselves at the center and on the edge. Organizations achieve unity by first experiencing disunity. It is the nature of the process. Change occurs at the top as well as at the bottom.

**Mergers and Collaboration:**

Merger and collaboration are broad terms used in all avenues of institutional realignment and as such require specific points of reference.

What is a merger? Simply put, it is the joining of two or more distinctive and separate entities into one central structure either by formally establishing a new organization or by integrating the operational components of the participating bodies.

What is collaboration? It is two or more groups working together in areas of common interest without creating a legal or formal institutional connection.

Before institutions can approach such types of structural and program realignments, they must first define their respective **missions** (what do we stand for?). Then it is essential that all parties revisit their particular **goals** (what are our purposes and roles?) and their specific institutional **visions** (how do we hope to shape our organization and where do we see it moving in the months or years ahead?). Organizations need to ask themselves, **"Where do we want to be at the end of the change process?"** Change is most successful when all parties involved in the transitions are directly committed and continuously included in the process.

Five key elements drive most mergers and collaborative endeavors:

1. shared values and common outcomes;
2. perceived benefits;
3. the capacity to achieve goals otherwise unrealized;
4. the best use of resources, personnel, etc.; and,
5. the desire to promote new working models.

One can describe three stages of institutional realignment. First, the merging organizations experiment with institutional cooperation. In this model, they enter into joint programs and share use of staff, space, and other resources. Second, participating institutions develop shared initiatives, such as coming together to promote new projects. Finally, the third model is the creation of a totally new organization. It is designed to encompass collective concerns of the two groups or the community. Regardless of the model, it is important to remember that in all negotiations there are institutional tradeoffs. Each party must know what it views as essential for any merger or collaborative arrangement to succeed and what it is prepared to discard.

Within any merger process, there is the constant reminder that when there is change, there is loss; all transitions bring various degrees of dislocation. In addition, as one enters into and moves through the process of institutional transitioning, leaders need to incorporate opportunities to evaluate the experience and its impact upon stakeholders.

In the literature associated with mergers and collaborative initiatives, there are critical cultural and organizational challenges as well:

- Initial periods of distrust and disruption (What will happen?)
- Relationship questions (How will the different players' interact with one another?)
- Power sharing issues (Who has it and how will it be shared and applied?)
- Realignment of assignments and tasks that may require on-going negotiations (What has changed and how well are we managing the new responsibilities?)

David LaPiana (1997) identified a number of roadblocks to effective consolidation. These included:

- loss of autonomy;
- failure to take into account the self-interests of key parties (managers, staff and board members); and,
- culture clash.

Our interviews confirmed that these roadblock factors were evident. It is evident that the merger has been hampered by the inability of the partners to create a new shared culture. This contributed to the initial difficulties in effectuating a satisfactory merger. The perceived "loss of autonomy" experienced by many participants involved the new structure's inability to protect the special interests of overseas advocates and to promote the particular needs of community proponents.

One theme which becomes clear throughout modern managerial literature is the idea that there must be the proper balance of input and sharing of power and tasks in accordance with the skills and talents of the respective merger partners. This is a major facet associated with organizational learning and institutional change and cannot be overstated.

(Mattessich and Monsey, 1992) suggest that six core factors are essential to successful mergers. Within each of these categories, are isolated specific "factors" that can contribute to or impede the integration process. We attempt to reference these core elements in our findings:

1. **Environment**: the history of collaboration and cooperation within the community.

2. **Membership:** Characteristics, mutual respect and trust, shared self-interest, and capacity to compromise.

3. **Process/Structure:** members share a stake in both the process and outcome, multiple layers of decision-making, flexibility, adaptability and clear roles and policy guidelines.

4. **Communication**: open and frequent communication and informal and formal lines of communication.

5. **Purpose:** concrete and attainable goals, shared vision, and unique purpose.

6. **Resources:** sufficient funds and a skilled convener.

# APPENDIX V – INTRODUCTION TO THE KETARIM MODEL

The governance model of the *Ketarim* (the three crowns) is based upon forms of Jewish governance that have existed throughout the history of Jewish people. Daniel Elazar and Stuart Cohen (1981) helped to frame this political model. They identified and defined the three Crowns: Torah, *Kehunah* and *Malchut*. Each can be understood both metaphorically and literally, depending upon one's own understanding of God. Central to the whole premise of the Crowns is the idea that the Jewish community operates as a polity, a form of government for Jewish people, however loosely this concept may be conceived. It was framed by an acceptance of the centrality of community and covenant. Using the Three Crowns (*Ketarim*) model in tandem with the literature on mergers provides a distinctive Jewish dimension that is necessary to understand the merger process and the evolution of the UJC.

*Keter "Kehunah"* originally referred to the priesthood before the destruction of the Second Temple and the subsequent permutations of those who came to serve the Jewish people. They were charged with the responsibility of guarding, interpreting and applying God's Law. In contemporary times, the communities' professional leadership fulfills these roles.

*Keter "Malchut"* symbolized the kings who ruled in the secular realm during the Biblical period. In our era, with the reestablishment of the State of Israel, coupled with the increased secularization of Jewish life in both Israel and the Diaspora, there has been a renewed focus on *Keter Malchut*. While this Crown is seen as the most dominant force in contemporary times, now it is being challenged by the representatives of the *Keter* Torah, in the form of the Israeli rabbinic establishment. In the Diaspora, lay leadership is seen as the contemporary counterparts.

In theory, each of the *Ketarim* is seen as equal, yet in practice there have been shifts in balance or influence among them throughout Jewish history. According to Elazar, "each *Keter* is to be regarded as a mediating institution between God and the *edah* (community) in possession of a different focus, thereby enabling each to exercise a constitutional check on the others." (Elazar,1997). Elazar further reminds us that no Jewish community is "constitutionally complete unless it contains representatives of all three *Ketarim* in one form or another." Through the millennia, as Jewish fortunes and realities changed, permutations were necessary. Eventually, a system of "checks and balances" evolved regarding the application of what was seen to be Jewish law, its guardians, and implementers. In the past, this system of checks and balances generally insured that no single group dominated Jewish life. There was always an attempt to keep the governance mechanisms responsive to the Jewish people and to insure that consent played an essential role in sustaining the balance of power among these sectors. Throughout the course of Jewish history, this balance would unravel.

Following the destruction of the Temple and the elimination of the Priesthood and the remnants of Jewish royalty, there evolved a series of new models of governance. According to Elazar, these emerge in different forms every 350 years or so, following a cataclysmic event affecting the Jewish people. In these instances, various groups (rabbis, functionaries and powerful Jews) revised the structures of community governance that, in turn, maintained a balance of power among these groups.

In contemporary times, the three crowns are symbolized through the contributions of rabbis and intellectuals who continue the tradition of transmitting values and knowledge to the Jewish community, communal professionals who provide core skills and expertise, and finally the *Parnassim*, the wealthy who offer both influence and affluence, while serving Jewish life as volunteers.

More recently, professionals have often collaborated in tilting the balance of authority in favor of the *Parnassim*, further isolating those voices representing the other key participants within the communal system. History suggests that in the long run this loss of balance does not serve the interests or well-being of the Jewish people. Consequently, we believe that it is important to utilize the *Ketarim* model in evaluating the future of Jewish organizational life, and more particularly, with reference to the potential success of the UJC.

With the advent of the State of Israel, the three crowns have taken on publicly legislated roles and incorporated the separation of powers. In countries outside of the United States, the structures still encourage the inclusion of the intellectual and political voices as well as those who are affluent and active in Jewish life. In the American context, it remains both essential and possible for some (other than the wealthy) to engage in the governance aspects of Jewish life. The same is certainly true in Israel both within the political system through elections, party politics, contending ideologies, and through the governance system of JAFI.

# *APPENDIX VI – THE KEHILLA MODEL*

Historically, as Jewish communities evolved after the dispersion, they developed the notion of what Elazar calls kinship and consent. Jewish communities, wherever they were, and however they were constructed, still believed in some kind of interdependent relationship agreed upon by the Jewish people. People living within those communities gave consent to those who would govern. However these communities were structured, there was a balance of powers between those who had wisdom and knowledge and those who had economic or secular power. Within that framework, structures evolved with parliamentary forms of one kind or another, with sanctions and services, which served and shaped Jewish life.

After the dispersion of the Jewish people, the governments which ruled the Jews decided on the degree to which self-governance would be allowed. Jews as individuals possessed few rights. The government decided its demands and imposed them upon the community at large. It became the responsibility of the Jewish communities to fulfill the government's expectations regarding tax collection, providing soldiers, keeping order, and the like.

The Covenantal idea is the underpinning of these community structures. The basis of our educational and social service infrastructures can be traced back to Biblical injunctions. This complex system involved courts that would apply sanctions, institutions that would provide for the poor and elderly, and governance structures that would appoint representatives to interact with non-Jewish communities and governments. The Jewish people were generally served well by these various structures.

The Kehilla model, (the word drawn from Kahal–community) evolved as the corporate structure under which Jews lived. Gemeinde is the word used to describe the communities which evolved under German rule. Pre-emancipation, the Jews were required to remain in the Jewish community unless they converted to the major religion. These background comments describe the Jews of Europe, although counterparts existed in the Arab world.

The end result was that the Jewish community was able to develop internal community structures which encompassed educational, judicial, social service, burial, religious and in some instances police systems within their own communities.

In many communities, the government under which Jews lived became the vehicle for the collection and distribution of monies that would benefit the communal enterprise. If a Jew "joined" the community after the Emancipation, a portion of his income was deducted by the government and returned to the community to provide for basic religious and communal services. This model continues today, with some permutations, in most Jewish communities throughout the world.

# APPENDIX VII – HISTORY OF SCHOOLS OF JEWISH COMMUNAL SERVICE

In 1907, the New York *Kehilla* sponsored the first program solely devoted to developing professionals. This experiment was short-lived. A program sponsored by Hebrew Union College in 1914 also failed for lack of support. From 1925 to 1940, Felix Warburg supported the Jewish School of Social Work in New York. It supplied a significant number of professionals for the field of Jewish communal service. Upon his death, the school closed due to a lack of funding. There was another hiatus before the Training Bureau for Jewish Communal Service was created in 1947. JDC, CJF and the National Jewish Welfare Board (now Jewish Community Centers of North America) supported the Training Bureau. The program received insufficient funding and closed in 1951.

# *EPILOGUE*

The contemporary literature on mergers and models of collaboration which we have introduced into this study (See Appendix II) provides helpful measures and standards by which one can assess the viability and success of such activities. This material has been included by the authors as one of the frameworks for evaluating our case study.

We identified in this literature a number of relevant themes. We noted that four core ideas were particularly significant in assessing why some of the participants in our study found both the merger process and the ultimate outcome problematic. Experts writing on the best practices associated with mergers suggest that shared communications represented a critical element in driving such a process. Here, all the key stakeholders were fully briefed on each component of the merger negotiations, while at the same time being given the opportunity to provide input.

A second essential ingredient involved the element of trust and open engagement. Successful mergers are directly linked to the level of candor associated with the discussions around merger.

The idea of tangible and early wins has been identified as another principle basic to the ultimate success of such endeavors.

Finally, each party to the merger must believe that in the end they were able to preserve those core non-negotiable organizational components that they perceived as essential for their institution to successfully participate in creating any new infrastructure.

# BIOGRAPHY OF AUTHORS

Gerald (Jerry) Bubis was the founding director of the School of Jewish Communal Service at Hebrew Union College-Jewish Institute of Religion, Los Angeles and the Alfred Goltschalk Professor of Jewish Communal Studies from 1968 to 1989. A consultant and author, he serves on many boards of directors and advisory councils — locally, nationally and internationally. Prior to entering academia, he served primarily in Jewish community centers but also in Hillel, federation, and camping settings for over 18 years. He has written extensively on the Jewish family, Jewish identity, Israel-diaspora relations, synagogues, and governance issues in Jewish life.

Steven Windmueller is the director of the School of Jewish Communal Service and Adjunct Associate Professor in Jewish Communal Studies at Hebrew Union College-Jewish Institute of Religion. He has held that post for nearly a decade after serving for a similar period of time as the executive director of the Jewish Community Relations Committee of the Los Angeles Jewish Federation. He took that post after having served as executive director of the Albany New York Jewish Federation. Prior to that, he served as a staff person of the American Jewish Committee. He received his Ph.D. from the University of Pennsylvania. He has written extensively on Jewish political behavior and communal trends and practice, among other themes.

# REFERENCES AND BIBLIOGRAPHY

Accel-team.com. (2001). *Employee motivation in practice.* Retrieved on April 21, 2003, from: http://www.accel-team.com/motivation/practice_00.html

Aronson, R. P. (1998). *A Statement of collective responsibility.* New York: United Jewish Communities (UJC).

Barkat, A. (2003, February 25). Jewish Agency gets first woman chair. *Haaretz.com, English edition.* Retrieved on February 25, 2003 from http://www.haaretzdaily.com/hasen/pages/ShArt.jhtml?itemNo=26 6366...

Berger, P. S. (May 22, 1998). *Letter to Dr. Steve B. Nasatir, President of Jewish federation of metropolitan Chicago regarding materials from Jewish Agency for Israel's (JAFI) task force on strategic planning.* Washington, DC: Author.

Bernstein, P. (1983). *To dwell in unity: The Jewish federation movement in America since 1960.* Philadelphia: The Jewish Publication Society of America.

Bloom, M. H. (1980, September 9). *Demographic changes and their effect on the campaign.* Delivered in San Francisco, CA, September 9, 1980.

Bloom, M. H. (1983, July 25). *Presentation at United Jewish Appeal (UJA) leadership retreat, Rye, New York – July 25, 1983.* UJA, New York, NY.

Bloom, M. H. (1984, February 9). *Memo to S. B. Horowitz, I. S. Blaustein, J.S. Friedman, R.A. Pearlman, D. Hersch, and M.A. Shorr regarding budget priorities.* New York: UJA.

Bloom, M. H. (1984, June 8). *Memo to Stanley B. Horowitz regarding leadership development/standardization of committees.* New York: UJA.

Bloom, M. H. (1984, July 20). *Memo to Victor Gelb regarding outline for study of Israel operation.* New York: UJA.

Bloom, M. H. (1984, August 2). *Memo to The Record regarding international leadership reunion in South Africa – Conversation with Irwin Field.* New York: UJA.

Bloom, M. H. (1984, August 24). *Background paper: Committee on scope and function of the UJA.* New York: UJA.

Bloom, M. H. (not dated). *Outline and notes for a communication by Mel Bloom (speech, position paper, article) to American Jewish fundraising professionals.* Unpublished manuscript.

Borden, L.M. & Perkins, D.F. (1999). Assessing your collaboration: A Self-evaluation tool. *Journal of Extension, 37*(2), retrieved on March 18, 2002 from http://www.joe.org/joe/1999april/tt1.html

Bubis, G., Elazar, D., & Silberman, M. *The Application of Jewish Political Theory to Jewish Communal Practice.* Jerusalem Center for Public Affairs, 1997.

Cardin, S. S. (1998, March). *Letter sent to members of United Israel Appeal (UIA) Board regarding the March 31, 1998 Board meeting to discuss the merger with Council of Jewish Federations (CJF) and UJA.* New York: UIA.

Cardin, S. S. (1998, April 6). *Memo sent to Members of UIA's Board of Directors and members of UIA's Board of Trustees regarding UIA and the partnership with CJF and UJA.* New York: UIA.

Cardin, S. S. (2003, January 24). Ill UJC needs second opinion. *Forward*. Retrieved on January 31, 2003 from http://www.forward.com/issues/2003/03.01.24/oped2.html

Cattan, N. (2003). *UJC launches search*. Retrieved on October 17, 2003 from http://www.forward.com/issues/2003/03.10.17/news16.ujc.html

Chronicle of Philanthropy 2/26/03, p. 33. (2003). Retrieved on February 7, 2003 from http://www.momentmag.com/features/feat2.html

*Collective responsibility (revised draft)*. (1998). New York: UJC.

*Collective responsibility (draft)*. (1998). New York: UJC.

Collins, J. Good to Great. HarperCollins Publishers, 2001.

Committee on Study of National Structure. (Date unknown). *Presentation on study of merger including pros and cons*. New York: UJC.

Conlin, M. & Hempel, J. (2003, December 1). The top givers: Today's philanthropists aren't leaving the good works to future generations – they're making their mark now. *Business Week*, 79-81.

CJF & UJA. (1996, June 26). *Recommendation for a new working partnership between the CJF and the UJA, Israel: June 26, 1996*. New York: UJC.

Davis, M. (editor). (1994). UJA *Memoirs: Irving Bernstein: An Oral History Anthology*. Jerusalem: Hebrew University

Delta Consulting Group, Inc. (1999, January 13). *Making Change Successful at Newco: Steering Group Kick-off Meeting* (power point presentation). Occoquan, VA.

Delta Consulting Group, Inc. (1999, April). *Overall Means, Gaps, and Top Priority Ratings* (power point presentation). Occoquan, VA.

Delta Consulting Group, Inc. (1999, April). *Populating Newco's Governance Structure* (power point presentation). Occoquan, VA.

Delta Consulting Group, Inc. (1999, June). *UJC Change Management and Consulting Support Requirements* (power point presentation). Occoquan, VA.

The Drafting Committee for the New Entity. (1999, February 5). *Documents for Newco*. New York: UJC.

Elazar, D.J. & Cohen, S. (1981), helped to frame the *Three Crowns: Torah, Kehunah and Malchut.*

Elazar, D. J. (1995). *Community & Polity: The Organizational Dynamics of American Jewry.* Philadelphia: The Jewish Publication Society.

*"The Four Tools: Local Collaborative Assessment of Capacity"* (2002). http://hdcs.fullerton.edu/cc/tools.htm

Freedman, R. (1983, March 22). *Job description and qualifications of the executive vice-chairman and executive vice-president.* New York: UJA.

"The future of Jewish Fund Raising" A Panel discussion. (1979, November). *Moment Magazine,* reprint.

Gartner, L.P. (1982). "The Midpassage of American Jewry, 1929 – 1945" in *American Jewish History, Edited* by Jeffrey S. Gurock, pp. 1 – 16. New York: Routledge.

Vaughan, P. A. (2002). *Mergers, Acquisitions, and Corporate Restructuring* (3rd. edition). New York: Wiley.

Geber, B. A. (2000). *"United Jewish Communities: A New Paradigm for Collaboration",* http://www.shma.com/mar00/geber.htm

Gidron, B. & Hasenfeld, Y. (1994). "Human Service Organizations and Self-Help Groups: Can They Collaborate?" *Nonprofit Management & Leadership,* 5(2), 159 – 172.

Giles, C., Wexler, R., Kraar, M., & Moscovitz, B. (Jun 11, 1998). *Memo sent out to Federation Presidents and Executives regarding the July 7 – 8, 1998 retreat.* New York: UJC.

Goldberg, A.J. (March 19, 1998). *Letter addressed to Jane Sherman in response to the minutes from the United Israel Appeal (UIA)-JAFI contract review committee meeting of January 26, 1998.* Boston: Combined Jewish Philanthropies.

Golensky, M. & DeRuiter, G.L. (2002). "The Urge to Merge: A Multiple-Case Study." *Nonprofit Management & Leadership* 13(2), 169 – 186.

Greilsheimer, L. B. (1998, May 19). *Memo to the CJF/UJA Partnership regarding the report based on retreat of large city presidents and executives – 13 of the 19 cities present.* New York: UJC.

Hammer, M. (2000, March). "Reengineering the UJC". *Sh'ma,* 30, pp. 3 – 4.

Himmelman, A. T. (1994). *Introduction to Designing a Collaborative,* Minneapolis, MN. (1406 West Lakes, Suite 209, Minneapolis, MN 55408).

Himmelrich, B.L., Friedman, D.D., Metzger, M., Meier, R. B., Schrayer, R. M. Nasatir, S. B., & et al. (1998). *A letter written to the Presidents and Executive Vice Presidents of the Council of Jewish Federations (CJF) and the United Jewish Appeal (UJA) expressing support for the merger.* New York: UJC.

Hoffman, H. G. & Klein, J. L. (August 4, 1998). *Letter written to Dr. Conrad L. Giles (President, CJF) and Mr. Richard L. Wexler (President, UJA) regarding their request for input on the upcoming merger of the two organizations as presented at a retreat July 7 – 8, 1998.* West Palm Beach, FL: Jewish Federation of Palm Beach County.

Hoffman, S. (2003, July 18). Friday morning…18 Tammuz 5763…July 18, 2003. *Weekly E-mail sent to the United Jewish Communities (UJC) e-mail list* [on-line serial].

Hoffman, S. (2003, August 1). Friday morning…3 Av 5763…August 1, 2003. *Weekly E-mail sent to the United Jewish Communities (UJC) e-mail list* [on-line serial].

Horowitz, S. B. (1987, March 26). *UJA's Second 50 years: A Fresh Program Portfolio* (draft). New York: UJA.

Hubbard, N. (2001). *Acquisition Strategy and Implementation* (revised edition). New York: Palgrave.

JAFI. (March 26, 1998). *A Background to the Jewish Agency for Israel (for Task Force Members) New* York: JAFI.

Karp, A. J. (1981). *To Give Life: The UJA in the Shaping of the American Jewish Community.* New York: Schocken Books.

Kohm, A. (2002). "What Happens When Nonprofits Consolidate (either partially or all the way)?" *Nonprofit World, 20*(3), 24 – 29.

Kolker, J. (Chairman). (1998). *Report of the Partnership Committee on Needs Assessment Process.* New York: UJC.

LaPiana, David (1997). *Beyond Collaboration: Strategic Restructuring for Nonprofit Organizations.*

LaPiana, David (2000). The Merger Workbook.

Managers Edge (1998) ISSN #1093-6157, page 8.

Marder, J. (1998, January). *Collaboration and Partnership: Presentation to Jewish Communal Professionals.* Presented at Jewish Communal Service Association of Southern California Annual Conference in Los Angeles, CA.

Mattessich, P. W. & Monsey, B. R. (1992). *Collaboration: What Makes It Work – A Review of Research Literature on Factors Influencing Successful Collaboration.* St. Paul, MN: Amherst H. Wilder Foundation.

Collaboration: What Makes it Work, Paul Mattessich and Barbara Monsey, Amherst H. Wilder Foundation, 1992.

McCormick, D. H. (2001). *Nonprofit Mergers: The Power of Successful Partnerships,* Gaithersburg, MD: Aspen Publishers.

McLaughlin, C. (1996). *Mergers & Consolidations* http://www.npccny.org/info/goi4.htm

McLaughlin, T. A. (1997). "Collaborating to Compete: Altruism Has Nothing to Do with Survival" *The NonProfit Times, July 1997,* p. 20.

McLaughlin, T. A. (1998). *Nonprofit Mergers and Alliances: A Strategic Planning Guide.* New York: Wiley.

Mendelsohn, E. (2000, March). "UJC: An Opportunity for Change". *Sh'ma*, 30, p. 9.

Meyerhoff, J. (Chairman). (1978, March 29). *Report of Committee on Review of the Management of the UJA, Inc.* New York: UJA.

*Minutes of the UIA Executive Committee.* (1999, January 11). New York, NY.

*Minutes of the UIA Executive Committee.* (1999, January 15). New York, NY.

Nasatir, S. B. (2000). *A Sense of our Past – A Vision for the Future – the Case of a Strong National Federated System.* Address at the UJC General Assembly, November 13, 2000. New York: UJC.

Nasatir, S. B. & Kent, D.P. (1999). *Proposal to Establish a United Jewish Federation.* Chicago: Jewish Federation of Metropolitan Chicago.

Newco. (1999, February). *A New Era in Jewish Community Life.* New York: UJC.

*The Nonprofit Merger Workbook.* (2001) St. Paul, MN: Amherst H. Wilder Foundation.

Oakley, E. (1994). *Enlightened leadership: Getting to the Heart of Change.* New York: Fireside.

O'Neil, M.S. (1999). *"Build the Latest Trends into your Planning". Nonprofit World, 17*(6), 45-46.

*On the Road to Merger.* (date unknown) Power Point Presentation presented to CJF, UJA, and UIA Leadership.

*Operational Plan: Integration of United Israel Appeal into Newco* (fourth draft). (1999, February 3). New York: United Israel Appeal.

Partnership Joint Operating Subcommittee on Community Service/Regionalization. (1998). *CJF-UJA Joint operating partnership: A Work Plan for the New Model of Service Delivery to the UJA-Federation System.* New York: UJC.

Peck, J. S. (2000, March). "A Culture of Community". *Sh'ma*, 30, pp. 11-12.

Pomerance, R. (2003). *"JDC Upsets Federation System with Appeal for Emergency Funds,"* http://jta.org/page_print_story.asp?inarticleid=12500&incategoryid

Pomerance, R. (2003, January 21). "With Growing Overseas Needs, UJC is pushing for greater funds." *JTA Daily News Bulletin, 81*(13), 1 – 2.

Pomerance, R. (2003, June 10). Head of federation system unveils long-awaited vision *JTA Daily News Bulletin.*

*Proposed Scope of Work (Draft).* (1998). New York: UJC.

Raphael, M. L. (1982). *A History of the United Jewish Appeal 1939 – 1982.* Providence, RI: Brown University.

Raye, B. (1992, September). *"Working Together Rather Than Working Alone – A Collaboration Model", Amherst* H. Wilder Foundation Management Support Services, St. Paul, MN.

Rayman, P. (2000, March). "Toward Responsive Accountability". *Sh'ma*, 30, pp. 10-11.

*"Recommendation for the Creation of a Joint Operating Partnership Between UJA and CJF,"* April 1997. New York: UJC.

*"The Road to Merger: Addressing the Governance Structure,"* July 1998. New York: UJC.

Rukin, M.B. & Shrage, B. (May 5, 1998). *Letter to Dr. Conrad L. Giles.*

Sample, S. B. (2002). *The Contrarian's Guide to Leadership.* CA: Jossey-Bass.

Sachar, H. (1990). *The Course Of Modern Jewish History.* NY: Random House.

Scheingold, C. (2000, March). The United Jewish Communities: Can Politics Keep Pace with Change? *Sh'ma, 30,* 570, pp. 1 – 2.

Schneirov, M. (May 11, 1998). *Memo to all task force invitee regarding strategic planning task force guidelines.* New York: JAFI.

Shrage, B. (1997, December 24). *Memo to Large City Presidents and Executives Regarding Federations Relationships to Israel.* Boston: Combined Jewish Philanthropies.

Shrage, B. (1999, July 26,). *Memo to Stephen H. Hoffman Regarding Jewish Agency Strategic Plan.* Boston: Combined Jewish Philanthropies.

Shrage, B. (2000, March). "Common Sense", *Sh'ma*, 30, pp. 7 -9.

Siegel-Itzkovich, J. (1984, November 2). "Meeting Jewish Needs: Judy Siegel-Itzkovich Talks to the New Head of the UJA, Stanley Horowitz" *The Jerusalem Post,* p. 6.

Solender, S. D. (2000, March). "A View from the Inside", *Sh'ma*, 30, pp. 15-16.

Solomon, J.R. (1998, July 29). *Memo to Marvin Lender and Bruce Soll Regarding Goals and Objectives of the Meeting to be Hosted by Leslie Wexner and Facilitated by David Nadler.* New York: The Andrea and Charles Bronfman Philanthropies.

Solomon, J.R. (1998, August 24). *Memo to Conrad Giles, Alan S. Jaffe, Marvin Lender, and Richard Wexler Regarding Merger Technical Assistance Project.* New York: The Andrea and Charles Bronfman Philanthropies.

Solomon, J.R. (2000, March). "Beyond Politics: Changing the Jewish Organization Scene", *Sh'ma*, 30, pp. 5 – 6.

Solomon, J.R. & Wachsstock, S.H. (2002). "Reflections on the UJC Merger: Issues Faced and Lessons Learned", *Journal of Jewish Communal Service*, *79*(1), 23 – 27.

Stock, E. (1987). *Partners and Pursestrings: A History of the United Israel Appeal.* Lanham, MD: United Press of America, Inc.

Stone, M. M., Bigelow, B., & Crittenden, W. (1999). "Research on Strategic Management in Nonprofit Organizations: Synthesis, Analysis, and Future Directions" *Administration & Society, 31*(3), 378 - 423.

Tisch, J. (2003). "Perfect? No. But UJC is a Success Story" *Forward* http://www.forward.com/issues/2003/03.01.31/oped3.html

Trimbath, S. (2002). *Mergers and Efficiency: Changes Across Time.* Boston: Kluwer Academic Publishers.

United Israel Appeal (UIA) (1997). *1996 – 1997 Annual Report.* New York.

UIA. (1998, January 14). *Activities Unique to the United Israel Appeal.* New York.

UIA. (1998, March 24). *UIA's Responsibilities within the Context of the Partnership.* New York.

UIA. (1998, June 9). *United Israel Appeal, Minutes of the Meeting of the Board of Directors, Tuesday, June 9, 1998, New York City* (draft). New York.

UIA. (1999, January 11). *Minutes of the UIA Executive Committee, January 11, 1999.* New York.

UIA. (1999, January 15). *Minutes of the UIA Executive Committee, January 15, 1999.* New York.

UIA. (1999, February 3). *Operational Plan: Integration of United Israel Appeal into Newco.* New York.

UIA. (1999, February 4). *Minutes of the UIA Executive Committee, February 4, 1999.* New York.

UJA. (1982, March 8). *Report to the National Officers of the United Jewish Appeal from its Long Range Planning Committee.* New York.

UJA. (1983, March 14). *Minutes from the UJA's Board meeting.* New York.

UJA. (1984, July 25). *UJA/Issues Briefing Paper: UJA Funds and Religious Pluralism in Israel.* New York.

UJA. (1984, July 26). *Notes for Report on International Meeting in South Africa.* New York.

UJC. (1999). *Executive Summary: The Role of Planning in the National System.* New York.

UJC. (2001, Spring). *United Jewish Communities: The Federations of North America.* New York.

UJC. (2001, July). *UJC Speaks.* New York.

UJC. (2001). *Resolution: Appointment of UJC Executive Committee.* From UJC, Inc. Board of Trustees Annual Meeting November 11, 2001. Includes List of UJC Executive Committee Members and Meeting Schedule. New York.

UJC. (2003, January 14). *United Jewish Communities Statement.* http://www.ujc.org/content_display.html? Article ID, 68730

UJC. (2003, September 5). *Findings and Recommendations: Work Groups on Social Welfare Outside of Israel.* New York.

UJC. (2003, October 20). *Report and Recommendations: Israel Work Group.* New York.

UJC. (2003, October 28). *Proposed Principles and Recommendations: ORT Work Group.* New York.

UJC. (2003, November 25). *Aliyah and Initial Klitah Work Group: Draft Report.* New York.

UJC. (2004, March 10). *Draft Resolution: ONAD.* New York.

UJC. (2004, March 18). *Uses of collective core funding: An Overview.* New York.

UJC. (2004, April). *Key Concepts: Overseas Allocations.* New York.

UJC. (date unknown). *United Jewish Communities: Who are we?* (press release). New York: Author.

Weber, S. (1996/1997). "Interagency and Multidisciplinary Collaboration: A Win-win Strategy", *Journal of Jewish Communal Service,* Winter/Spring 1996/97, 233 – 242.

Wexler, R. (2002). *"United Jewish Catastrophes...A Love Story",* unpublished manuscript.

Wexler, R. (2002, December 27). "Rebuild the Foundation of North American Jewry's Central Address", *Forward,* p.9.

Windmueller, S. (2002) *"Re-Envisioning the Jewish Federation",* Los Angeles (unpublished).

Yankey, J.A., Wester, B., & Campbell, D. (1998). "Managing Mergers and Consolidations" in National Association of Social Workers, Inc. (Ed.), *Skills for Effective Management of Nonprofit Organizations* (pp. 492 – 503), Washington, DC: NASW Press.

Yoffie, E. H. (1998, January 12). Letter Written to Leadership of CJF and UJA Expressing Concern about the Merger and their Relationship with the Conservative and Reform Movements. New York: (URJ) UAHC.

Accountants, 21, 66, 134, 136, 153

CJF, 2, 5, 8, 10, 17, 18, 21, 22, 25, 26, 27, 30, 31, 32, 35, 37, 38, 41, 44, 47, 48, 49, 50, 56, 59, 62, 65, 67, 68, 71, 72, 74, 78, 79, 80, 103, 107, 114, 147, 151, 152, 154, 155, 158, 159, 163

Classifications, 1, 21, 65

Federations, 2, 17, 19, 38, 45, 47, 59, 79, 92, 97, 151, 155, 159, 162

Governance and Structure, 21, 89, 134

Internationalists, 67

JAFI, 3, 13, 17, 18, 20, 21, 26, 27, 30, 31, 38, 42, 48, 49, 50, 66, 67, 74, 75, 76, 103, 104, 144, 150, 154, 155, 159

JDC, 1, 3, 10, 17, 19, 20, 21, 27, 33, 35, 38, 42, 50, 51, 66, 67, 72, 74, 75, 76, 79, 80, 107, 147, 158, 145, 142

Localists, 21, 65, 71, 76, 138

Professionals and Lay Leadership, 1, 42

Recommendations, 1, 88

Reflections, 1, 83, 87

UIA, 2, 5, 8, 10, 13, 17, 18, 21, 25, 26, 27, 31, 32, 34, 37, 38, 42, 43, 49, 55, 56, 59, 67, 68, 75, 76, 79, 80, 103, 114, 151, 154, 157, 158, 161, 163

UJA, 2, 5, 8, 10, 13, 17, 18, 19, 20, 21, 22, 25, 26, 27, 28, 29, 30, 31, 32, 33, 34, 35, 37, 38, 41, 42, 43, 44, 47, 48, 49, 50, 52, 53, 55, 56, 58, 59, 60, 61, 62, 66, 67, 68, 69, 70, 71, 72, 76, 78, 79, 80, 91, 103, 114, 150, 151, 152, 153, 154, 155, 157, 158, 159, 160, 161, 162, 163

UJC, 2, 3, 4, 5, 8, 12, 13, 15, 16, 17, 21, 27, 29, 30, 36, 37, 38, 39, 40, 41, 45, 46, 47, 48, 49, 51, 56, 60, 61, 62, 63, 69, 70, 71, 72, 73, 74, 75, 76, 79, 81, 83, 84, 85, 87, 89, 90, 92, 93, 94, 95, 96, 97, 98, 99, 101, 102, 103, 104, 105, 110, 112, 113, 134, 142, 144, 150, 152, 153, 154, 155, 156, 157, 158, 159, 160, 162, 163

Visionaries, 68

Winners, 1, 78